ABERDEEN — FINAL EDITION

Best wishes
Bob Crampsey

ABERDEEN —
FINAL EDITION

By

BOB CRAMPSEY

Keith Murray Publishing

ABERDEEN — FINAL EDITION
by
BOB CRAMPSEY

First published November 1990

ISBN 1 870978 30 7

Keith Murray Publishing
46 Portal Crescent
Tillydrone
Aberdeen AB2 2SP

Printed by Astra Printing Services, Aberdeen

ACKNOWLEDGEMENTS

It is my pleasure to acknowledge the help which I received from various people. Many Aberdeen players spoke to me, it was a particular delight to relive old campaigns with Willie Cooper, George Hamilton, Fred Martin, Jimmy Wilson, Bobby Clark, Willie Miller and Alex McLeish. I have to thank too the Pittodrie office staff for their unfailing cheerful response to my several enquiries and also the Board and manager Alex Smith for help freely given.

With regard to illustrations, I would like to thank the Aberdeen Press & Journal; Andy Allan, Picture Editor of the Daily Record and Sunday Mail; John McLennan of Edinburgh and All Sport UK Ltd. (Picture Agency).

Finally, I would like to thank Maggie Seaton for her tremendous efficiency in preparing the text and her excellent and well-received suggestions for its occasional improvement!

Bob Crampsey

CONTENTS

CHAPTER ONE

1937 v. CELTIC

OVERTURES AND BEGINNERS

There was just the slightest lightening of the sky as the earliest of the 17 special trains jerked its first few yards out of the Joint Station at 4.25 am on the last Saturday of April 1937. Aboard were some 600 souls, the majority of them from the city itself but with many intrepid spirits from the outlying districts who had come in to Aberdeen the previous night and hadn't bothered going home.

Their side, the Dons, had at the sixth attempt reached the final of the Scottish Cup and their opponents would be Celtic, less successful in the 1930s than their great rivals Rangers but in a peculiar way more glamorous. As the packed train sped south the red-eyed supporters shrugged off their tiredness in discussions on how Aberdeen had got to the final and what the day to come would bring.

It had been a curious progression to the Cup Final and Aberdeen had made comparatively little money from it, thanks to a strange quirk in the draw which had given them a bye as late as the third round. Ties against Inverness Thistle, Third Lanark and Hamilton Academical had brought respectable but far from enormous crowds (although 20,000 at Douglas Park for the Hamilton match was relatively extremely good) and then the semi-final against Morton had brought victory but scarcely wealth untold. The venue for this last match, Easter Road, strikes one as rather curious and was not the first choice of location which would give rise to heated complaints from North-Eastern quarters. Still, 32,000 was fair enough, Billy Strauss and Matt Armstrong had scored and there was the certainty of a six figure crowd when the train arrived at its Glasgow terminus, Buchanan Street.

A more important train had left the evening before. The team and official party had travelled down on the 5.25 pm and, at the moment of parting, a black cat had been presented to the little Irish skipper, Eddie Falloon. He proudly exhibited the lucky (or perhaps luckless) animal on the compartment table before the train slowly drew out, the good wishes of the 1,000 fans who had turned up at the station following them faintly down the line.

As they thundered towards Glasgow they passed dozens of buses bearing supporters from the small Buchan towns and villages. One bus operator was to claim "If I had had a hundred buses I could have filled them". The days of mass private motoring were not yet, but even at that the main Aberdeen to Glasgow road was much busier than it would normally have been on a Friday night.

For the great majority however the train was the indicated mode of transport and from early on the Saturday morning Buchanan Street was awash with black and gold favours. It would incidentally be the only time that these Aberdeen colours would make their appearance at a Scottish Cup final. The neighbouring restaurants, cafés, and those establishments which were so much of the Thirties, milkbars, were besieged by hungry Northerners who devoured according to the *Glasgow Herald* hundredweights of bacon and thousands of eggs. They were mostly hatted and wearing raincoats for the forecast had been quite uncertain and the overwhelming mass of Aberdeen supporters would end up on the open terracing. Thirty thousand of them, said the optimists, fifteen, declared the more conservative. In the end best estimates put the total of committed Dons supporters as being in the region of 20,000.

They would of course be in a minority, Aberdeen fans at Hampden always are, although they have at times been inclined to make rather too much of this. There is always a lot of passive goodwill when they play an Old Firm side in the final from the supporters of the other half of that concern who have not made the final in that particular year.

Glasgow was preparing for the Coronation of King George VI and Queen Elizabeth which would take place three weeks later and many of the Aberdeen menfolk found themselves under pressure from wives and girlfriends to have a look at the special window displays which the big Glasgow stores in Buchanan Street had mounted. The more percipient supporters risked feminine wrath by dourly insisting that they should get to Hampden straight away as there would be an enormous crowd and admission would be on the principle of first come first served. The heightening excitement was enough to make almost everyone forget the loss of a night's sleep.

The team of course had slept. They were quartered in St Enoch's Hotel, above another of the four mainline stations which Glasgow then possessed. After dinner they had been visited by two famous Rangers, Alan Morton and Bob McPhail who would be presumed to have passed on some not too disinterested hints on how to tackle Celtic. The pessimists in the Aberdeen party noted that on that same Friday evening Rangers had gone down to a Clyde side of quite modest ability.

That on the day the crowds were enormous, the author is in a splendid position to testify. He lived within 200 yards of the ground and although not allowed to go to the game, an eminently sensible prohibition on the twin grounds of age and height, he was permitted to go and collect cigarette cards and made a haul which put him into the millionaire class in that particular brand of primary schoolboy currency.

The presence of Aberdeen in the final and the accents which were attractive but strange to our untutored Western lugs imparted a special sense of occasion to this match. We had never seen so many ladies going to the football. My mother, out shopping on the Saturday morning, remarked on this and on the strength of it became a committed Aberdeen supporter for the day. From time to time outbursts of good-humoured cheering would issue from below the black and gold tammies and top hats, often for no very apparent reason.

The logistics in moving this vast throng from city centre to Hampden were staggering. Every four minutes a train arrived at Mount Florida station. On the Number 19 tram route —older Glaswegians still called it "the white car" - there were 65 trams per hour from Springburn and the north side of the city. From Govan (on a day when Rangers were not involved) there were 44 buses an hour on the 4A route. The Corporation Transport Department calculated that it was providing 16,600 tramcar seats to the hour and 7,800 bus places. On a loopline by the side of the Queen's Park Recreation Ground 80 trams sat ready to ferry away spectators as soon as the final whistle went.

It seemed as if all Aberdeen was there. Trawler owners, desperate to see the match, had instructed their skippers not to land catches on the Saturday. It would have been pleasant to record that such enthusiasm and sacrifice were universally rewarded, but it has to be said that the arrangements for the marshalling of the crowd were primitive and dangerous to a degree and that only a benign Providence prevented a catastrophe on the scale of the Ibrox Disaster of 1971.

The week before, the Scotland v. England match had been played at Hampden Park and although the official attendance had been given as above 149,000, there had been no serious incidents. The S.F.A. claimed that it was not possible to make arrangements for two all-ticket games on consecutive weeks and so entrance to the Cup Final degenerated into a free for all. In the event, 146,000 would find themselves inside Hampden Park but it seems clear that at least 30,000 of these saw little or nothing of the game. Not all were as unlucky as the anonymous Aberdonian who has given us this graphic account in the *Aberdeen Press and Journal* of April 26, 1937:

"There were 144,000 inside (opinions varied) at least 20,000 in the surrounding streets and open spaces and nobody knows how many more who turned back at the train and bus stations when they learned that it would be a waste of time going to the ground. In Somerville Drive the spectacle was terrifying. The street was packed with struggling humanity that looked like resolving itself into a jelly. Just then the gates were closed and there was a howl of rage.

"For my bob I had a magnificent view of the back of someone's neck. I could also see the time on the stand clock.

It was quite a good neck, clean and all that sort of thing, but not worth a bob to see. Still, I knew the time.

"There was a suggestion of demanding our money back but just then somebody scored and we all dashed back madly to see — the back of more necks.

"For our benefit somebody on the terracing barricade tried his hand at a running commentary but he was too temperamental; he had Celtic three up in the first ten minutes but the referee had seemingly not seen two of them.

"I decided I would like to see the match and after a little mild all-in wrestling got to the enclosure. A railing cut off the enclosure from the common herd, obscuring my view of the east goal and a third of the field."

Despite the determinedly light-hearted tone of this report, it is clear that the narrator had undergone an experience which was not only uncomfortable and dangerous but in the last resort fraudulent, since he had been admitted to a match which he had no reasonable expectation of seeing. There would be strong comments on this afterwards, but in the meantime the teams had taken the field and the game would get under way for the benefit of that considerable majority who could see what was about to happen.

The teams on that day formed up on lines which were familiar to every Scottish football follower of the day. Time has inevitably removed the players from the knowledge of younger supporters so it is worthwhile considering them in detail.

ABERDEEN: Johnstone; Cooper, Temple, Dunlop, Falloon, Thomson, Beynon, MacKenzie, Armstrong, Mills, Lang.

Of that side, the goalkeeper, George Johnstone, already had a Scottish Cup medal at Junior level, won with Benburb. Willie Cooper had for a decade been a stalwart in the Aberdeen side, unflurried, unspectacular, absolutely dependable. Left back Temple shared a common origin with deputy left winger Lang, in that both had come to Pittodrie from the pre-war Stirling senior club, King's Park. The wing-halves followed a well-known convention whereby Frank Dunlop was the hardier and George Thomson the silkier. They flanked the diminutive Irishman Eddie Falloon whose modest 5'5 " did not seem to impede his out-jumping taller opponents. The little Irishman's liking for cricket was shared by at least two other members of the side, Willie Cooper and centre-forward Matt Armstrong. Armstrong had a point to prove on this April day for he had been a provisional Celtic signing without ever making the transition to the permanent staff at Parkhead. At inside-left for the Dons was the graceful, classical Willie Mills, one of the famous footballing family from the Vale of Leven. It was therefore inevitable that he would list quoiting among his recreations.

There was one notable omission from the Aberdeen side, that of South African Billy Strauss at outside-left. He had been injured in that very same semi-final in which he had scored one of the two goals that had given the Dons victory against Morton.

CELTIC: Kennoway; Hogg, Morrison, Geatons, Lyon, Paterson, Delaney, Buchan, McGrory, Crum, Murphy.

Any side which met Celtic in a Scottish Cup final met not only eleven players but the most powerful and enduring of club legends. Though they would be inconsistent in the League — and here it should be noted that they had won the League the previous season and would do so again the year after this final — they did regard the Scottish Cup as their private property. Their manager, Willie Maley, had been associated with every Scottish Cup success the club had had, either as a player or manager, since 1890. It was EXPECTED that Celtic would at least reach the final every other year. For Maley's opposite number, Paddy Travers, reaching Hampden was of itself an enviable achievement.

Studying the Celtic line-up could have induced deep depression in opponents. Joe Kennoway in goal was one of the very few players, perhaps the only player, to have been capped by three separate countries, in his case Canada, the U.S.A. and Scotland. At right-back Bobby Hogg was yet another of the taken-for-granted key men that that position seemed to produce. Aberdeen, as has been noted, had one in Willie Cooper and Rangers another in Dougie Gray, an Aberdonian as it happened.

The Celtic skipper, Willie Lyon, was a commanding figure, recently joined from Queen's Park. He was English which meant that, for the collectors of statistical oddities, neither captain was a Scot. Up front Jimmy Delaney was a dasher by no means devoid of skill, Willie Buchan was a thoughtful, probing inside-forward whose loping stride masked

1937 ABERDEEN v. CELTIC. Goalmouth thrills in Cup Final.

Johnstone, Aberdeen's goalkeeper goes down to save at full-length from Buchan, in the Scottish Cup final between Aberdeen and Celtic at Hampden. Falloon is lying on the ground after an unsuccessful attempt to tackle, and Cooper and Temple are watching events anxiously.

considerable pace and at centre-forward in the green and white hoops lurked the redoubtable James Edward McGrory who would break every British goal-scoring record. He was at the end of his career now but perhaps there was one last hurrah left in him. Johnny Crum was a cool hand at finishing and on the left wing Frank Murphy completed a formidable quintet.

The preliminaries, more than usually tedious to those who had travelled overnight, were disposed of and the civically named referee, Mungo Hutton, set the match in motion. The author had three uncles, all Celtic supporters who, unlike him, were permitted to see the match. He grew up on their tales of a superlative Celtic display wearing down a skilful Aberdeen side but since then he has seen the film of the match and in truth it was fairly ordinary. Goalkeepers threw themselves not at the ball, they already had that, but to one side as the burly forwards of the day attempted to bury them in the back of the net. It was all perfectly good-tempered but the prevalence of the shoulder charge did not encourage a flourishing of skills.

For Aberdeen to win it was essential that each player played to his potential. On the day, to their own great disappointment, two key men, Willie Mills and George Thomson, did not. The importance of Mills to that Aberdeen side could scarcely be exaggerated. With an ominous prophetic instinct, an Aberdeen writer for the *Glasgow Evening Times*, bearing the unlikely nom de plume of A. Small Chunk of Granite, wrote:

"On his game he (Mills) is extremely difficult to stop, but when he fails to hit it off he can give the forward line a ragged and lop-sided look." And on the day he and Thomson played on top of each other so that much of the Aberdeen midfield momentum was lost.

So it proved and yet Aberdeen surmounted the potentially fatal shock of losing an early goal. McGrory fastened on to a free kick and shot for goal. The shot was not especially powerful but well-placed and George Johnstone could only turn it aside. As he did so he lost his footing and before he could regain it, little Johnny Crum (the normal bit players would be the stars of this particular final) had returned it to the net.

Aberdeen proceeded to prove, within a minute, that a side is never more vulnerable than in the period immediately after which it has scored. Again the goal, rapturously received,

1937 ABERDEEN v. CELTIC. Aberdeen right back Willie Cooper prepares to close down the legendary Celtic centre-forward Jimmy McGrory.

was of no great distinction. The little Welshman on the Dons' right wing, Jacky Beynon, crossed a ball which Lyon lunged at and partially unsighted Kennoway in goal. He in turn could only beat out a shot from Mills and Matt Armstrong netted a goal which must have given him abnormal satisfaction.

It could now have been thought that the initiative was with Aberdeen. In those less complicated days the club was actually at that very minute playing a Reserve match at Pittodrie against Kilmarnock and arrangements had been made to notify the spectators there by loudspeaker of the current state of play at Hampden. The first three such messages, delivered at 15 minute intervals, recorded the score at 1-1. So too the first message in the second half, but Aberdeen had never quite shaken off their nerves and the tide was flowing strongly towards George Johnstone's goal. It became increasingly more probable that a draw and a chance to do better the second time round were about the peaks of Aberdonian ambition.

With just twenty minutes to go in the match that hope was cut short. It came just after the substitute, Lang, had missed two very credible chances, shooting past on one occasion and allowing Kennoway to smother-save on the other. There was a tinge of controversy about the goal as the move started when McGrory bustled past Temple and it seemed just possible that he had used an arm to control the ball. There was the slightest of hesitations in the Aberdeen defence and that was all that Willie Buchan asked or needed. He was through at once and his low placed shot went in off the post. Here again legend was more dramatic than reality. My three uncles would have had it that the ball hit one post, ran along the line, paused momentarily, sneered at the Aberdeen goalkeeper and then crossed the line off the other post. In less poetic fact, the ball hit Johnstone's right-hand post and almost immediately crossed the line. The restrained congratulations of the Celtic forwards in the film are testimony of a more dignified world.

Now, when all seemed lost, Aberdeen roused themselves and the last few minutes saw them camped in Kennoway's area as they hoisted an aerial bombardment which saw the ball bob from head to head perilously close to the Celtic net. But the final, clearing head was always a Celtic one and as Mungo Hutton blew his whistle for the last time, the Cup was going to Parkhead.

As a first attempt, it had been very meritorious and both supporters and team had made many friends by their cheerful sporting approach and dignified acceptance of defeat. First to shake the hand of the referee was captain Eddie Falloon, and that is a gesture which is always infinitely more impressive when it comes from the leader of the vanquished. His own summing-up: "We lost in a fair fight" was admirably terse. Even *Man in the Know* writing for the Catholic paper *The Glasgow Observer* and not noted for the charity of his observations on opposing teams, was moved to say: "It was a pity that Aberdeen should be the victims. They were a clever and a sporting team." Not all press critics were as loud in their praises however. Writing in the *Evening Times*, 'Onlooker' thought that the Dons had suffered a bad collective case of nerves. His chief, 'Alan Breck' was disposed to agree: "The explanation is that Aberdeen are still learning to meet the really big occasions." Might the presence of Strauss have tipped things? Perhaps. The most influential players are always thought to be those who do not actually take part.

By general agreement the stars on the Aberdeen side had been Falloon and Johnstone and for Celtic Geatons (another quiet man), Buchan and Crum. It had been Buchan's last important match for Celtic as within six months he would be transferred to Blackpool. By the time Aberdeen and Celtic next met in a Scottish Cup final, Jimmy McGrory would be the Celtic manager.

Of the Aberdeen side that gave of their best unavailingly on that April day in 1937 three would know what it was to walk up for a winner's medal. The following year Paddy Travers would move to Clyde taking with him Eddie Falloon, and the Irishman would lead the Clyde team to victory in the last pre-war Scottish Cup Final, that of 1939. Before that, the Scottish Cup had been wrapped in black and gold ribbons but they were the colours of East Fife, not Aberdeen. The Fifers, in the Second Division then, overcame all odds to beat Kilmarnock in the replayed final of 1938. I would like to think that it was the presence of the author in the crowd which encouraged them. Aberdeen changed to the more mundane red shirts in 1939 and henceforth that would be the colour of the adorning ribbon when at last they won the Cup.

It was Willie Maley's ultimate Scottish Cup success

with Celtic and indeed Aberdeen would get their name on the trophy before the next inscription for Celtic was made. His chairman, Tom White, made the rather startling statement that Scottish football as a whole would have profited by an Aberdeen victory.

The post-match celebrations and commiserations did not totally obscure the serious flaws in the arrangements for spectators. In theory the crowd should have been easy to marshal, the North Stand was in use at a Scottish Cup final for the first time and it was reckoned (certainly over-optimistically) that each of the 117 turnstiles was capable of admitting 2,000 spectators per hour.

The *Glasgow Herald* was not to be mollified and was very severe on the instances of over-crowding:

"It was deemed unnecessary to issue tickets because those responsible for the arrangements under-estimated the numbers likely to attend ...... The International match proved that the all-ticket system had its limitations and it loses much of its value when the spectator's ticket admits him to any part of the terracing and not, as should be the case, to one particular section."

The Herald then went on to point out that the situation would have been infinitely more serious but for the great good nature of the crowd. There would never again be a crowd of quite that magnitude at a Scottish Cup final; the abiding image, once having seen the newsreel film of the match, is of how well-dressed and sedately behaved that huge assembly was.

At night the streets of Glasgow were gay with the black and gold favours of the Aberdeen supporters. Most of them were making for their trains or seeking to be re-united with their buses. For those who stayed on a little later there was a choice of entertainment. It seems improbable that too many of that afternoon's crowd would have ended up watching Anton Dolin and Alicia Markova dancing with the Ballet Markova but one never knows. A safer bet may have been as part of the audience which saw and heard Dave Willis top the bill at the Empire.

The team themselves had not lingered long after the match and had in fact arrived back in Aberdeen just after ten o'clock. In the large crowd which met them there was no suggestion of reproach for failure, rather encouragement for the following year and the feeling that a very creditable first attempt had been made that afternoon. It was recognised that football was a strange game. Were Celtic not, even now, at the Cup-winners dinner and had they not struggled desperately against Stenhousemuir at Ochilview in an early round of the competition?

The players went off to get over it and, if they could, enjoy themselves. The scorer of the goal, Matt Armstrong, was carried shoulder high and with his team-mate, George Thomson, dropped in at the local Palais de Danse where in response to public demand he made a speech of which the burden was "Wait till next year". It seemed as if the last word on the final would be the considered assessment of the *Glasgow Herald:* "The disinterested follower of the game (if that is not a contradiction in terms) must regret that the challengers have once again failed to distribute the spoils more freely throughout the country". There were however to be two tragic tail-pieces which affected Aberdeen football folk deeply.

On the day after the match, a member of the Aberdeen board, W.D. Hay, collapsed and died suddenly. He was a comparatively young man (50), had attended the Hampden match and gave every indication of being in excellent health and spirits. He had gone motoring on the Sunday afternoon and on returning home, he had collapsed and died. He was a member of the S.F.A. Council and was on the International Selection Committee, indeed he was about to go to Czechoslovakia for the forthcoming international with that country in Prague.

This was a grievous death, but within a few weeks came another which attracted public attention and public sympathy even more. Aberdeen had arranged to go to South Africa during the close season with a party of 16 players and four officials. Paddy Travers had always had strong links with the Union and he would preserve this connection when he moved on to take over Clyde. At an early stage in the tour Jacky Beynon, the Welshman who had set up the Aberdeen goal at Hampden, went down with appendicitis. He was visited by his team-mates in hospital but with shocking suddenness, peritonitis developed and he died and was buried thousands of miles from home. The tour had to proceed but the loss to the player's family and colleagues can easily be imagined.

Despite the sad consequences, the Cup Final of 1937 had been a great adventure. The club now knew that it could acquit itself with credit in the very last stage of a major national competition. Aberdeen would be back but only after a maniacal politician had turned the world upside-down.

1937 — WILLIE COOPER REMEMBERS

It was a great occasion, 1937, with tremendous excitement in the town. I was quite an experienced player by then, at the half-way point in my career in fact. I had come to Pittodrie from Mugiemoss in 1927 but before that time I had been a provisional signing. We trained two nights a week at Pittodrie while Juniors, and for that we got £1.

The manager was Paddy Travers, a very good manager although he did not take much if anything to do with the training and what would now be called tactics, I suppose. That was handled by the trainer, Donald Colman, and he was very astute. His real name was Cunningham but as a young man he had not wanted his parents to know that he was playing professional football and so he used the name Colman.

The final itself was a bit disappointing. I think the whole team was nervous. I had a good enough game against the Celtic winger Murphy but nothing out of the ordinary. It wasn't always the well-known wingers that gave you trouble. I still have the cutting from when I had a good game against the great Alan Morton, "Morton coopered!". Yet wee Jimmy Caskie of St Johnstone always gave me a lot of bother.

That day at Hampden we only really started to play with ten minutes or so left and us a goal down. We depended on Willie Mills a lot, our most talented forward, and he had a quiet game that day. We all did, I suppose. But then the crowd was over 140,000 and I don't suppose we'd ever played to even half that before. Jimmy McGrory was difficult to play against, all elbows and shoulders. Jimmy Delaney was fast and dashing but I always felt just a bit over-rated.

There were no medals for the losers in 1937, there are really only the newspaper reports to let me know I played. I remember more clearly than the final the tour of South Africa which took place immediately afterwards. We were away for almost three months, it took about ten days to sail there, I think, and another ten to come back. We sailed by Union Castle, we went out on the Stirling Castle and came back on the Athlone Castle. We played all over South Africa, Johannesburg, Cape Town, Durban, Bloemfontein. We had planned to take the Scottish Cup with us if we had beaten Celtic. It was all-white sides that we played. We were told that we could dribble round

23

them if we liked but not to make them look stupid by exhibition football, by which they meant passing among ourselves. Of course it was a wonderful experience, we went everywhere by train, but things were obviously never the same after poor Jacky Beynon died in hospital. Paddy Travers knew South Africa well and had been out there before.

About a year or so after that we changed from the black and gold jerseys — I thought they were very smart especially when they added the white collar — to the red jerseys that they still wear today. Shortly after that the war broke out and I went back to my trade as a marine engineer. Since I had then been playing senior football for more than twelve years, I thought that my career as a player was bound to be over.

CHAPTER TWO

1947 v. HIBERNIAN

A MEDAL FOR THE TWELFTH MAN

Ten years elapsed before Aberdeen took the field at Hampden again for a Scottish Cup final. Any decade would have seen great changes but one which had encompassed a World War was clearly even more far-reaching in its effects, although on the surface things seemed to have got back to normal to a remarkable degree.

The country was not so much devastated by war as almost terminally shabby. There had been a considerable amount of destruction and very little permanent building. The useful but unlovely "prefabs" sprouted on every side. Football grounds which had been on a minimal care and maintenance basis during the war were suddenly revealed as seriously inadequate when the crowds flocked back. There was an unparalleled hunger for the game, so that a Glasgow Cup final in 1949 between a good Third Lanark side and a mediocre Celtic one attracted the astonishing figure of 87,000 through the turnstiles.

Aberdeen had had a chequered war-time football history. All football had stopped in September 1939 but when the expected aerial onslaught did not arrive within hours or even months a wartime competition was arranged. This was a Regional League played in two sections, West and East, and

Aberdeen were allocated to an Eastern section which lacked the big Glasgow clubs or Motherwell. King's Park and Stenhousemuir were poor exchange for the Old Firm and Aberdeen lost heavily financially in the period between the creation of the Regional Leagues in October 1939 and the end of the season in May 1940. Just at the moment when there was a move to revert to the pre-war structure the Germans invaded France and the Low Countries. The Scottish Football League suspended operations for the duration of the war, giving groups of clubs the right to form regional leagues if they wished.

Since the Government wished to keep civilian and non-essential travelling to a minimum, this posed problems for Aberdeen, comparatively geographically isolated as they were. They could not expect an invitation to join the 16 club Southern League and they did not get one. All efforts to found a similar league in the North-East for season 1940-1941 foundered on the reluctance of the other two leading clubs in that area, Dundee and St Johnstone, to become involved in war-time football. The result was that for that season Aberdeen had no formal competitive existence and the prospect stretched before them of being out of football for the duration of the war.

That this did not happen was due not only to their own enthusiasm but to that of Dundee United, three of the Fife clubs (Cowdenbeath had been an early war-time casualty) and, less expectedly, to Rangers. The Ibrox club had taken war-time football seriously from the outset, in commendable contrast to Celtic, and they offered to keep a second team in being and play it in the North-Eastern League, as the new body was to be called.

This league, brought into existence in the most unpromising circumstances, would in many respects be quite visionary with its League cup-ties being decided over two legs and a differential points system being operated for home and away wins and draws. There was of course a strong element of improvisation about it all. Many pre-war players had gone off to the Services. Those who had not were often on work of national importance and were not always available. Players trained when and as they could.

Nevertheless, Aberdeen used war-time football wisely. Many distinguished names appeared on their team-sheet. The cultured Bobby Ancell of Newcastle United, who would later produce one of the purest-ever Scottish footballing sides at

Motherwell, turned out. So did Willie Lyon of Celtic who had done so much to thwart the 1937 Final Dons. So did one Stanley Mortensen, later to score a hat-trick in an F.A. Cup Final and so too did the incisively-tackling Sammy Cox, then with Queen's Park and later a Ranger. There were other players less well-known but extremely useful, such as the prolific-scoring Alec Gourlay of Partick Thistle who rarely left his uniform on his Pittodrie peg without going out and banging in a couple of goals.

There was some very good football played and people were appreciative of it in those grey war-time winters, but it was in every sense a marking of time until things could properly get under way again. In the interim season, a curious Limbo land was that of 1945-46. Aberdeen had won a major trophy at Hampden when they took the Southern League Cup — in a marvellous and cavalier disregard of geography — by defeating Rangers 3-2. It was a feat that properly lies outside the scope of this book but it was important in that a psychological barrier had been overcome and not only had Rangers been beaten, but they had been beaten after the Ibrox club had clawed its way back to 2-2 from two goals down.

Who would the returning serviceman or munitions worker have recognised as he stood on the terracing in those early days of 1947? Three of the 1937 Cup Final side were still regulars. George Johnstone was back in goal, having helped out Celtic for a spell during the war before falling out with both the Parkhead board and the S.F.A. George was never one to suffer fools gladly and he thought, however erroneously, that fools were to be found on both these bodies. Willie Cooper was there, a guarantee of continuity in an uneasily-changing world, and so too was Frank Dunlop. The pre-war influence did not end there for up front were two of the most popular players ever to wear an Aberdeen jersey. Archie Baird had had very little chance to establish himself before the war, since coming north from a Strathclyde team which included Willie Waddell, Neil McMenemy who had every senior club in Scotland after him but opted to stay junior, and Charlie Adam who for years was an outstanding winger with Leicester City. Archie's great days were to come whereas his colleague, George Hamilton, was already pretty well established when football came to a halt in 1939.

He had been signed from Queen of the South in 1938 and

1937/47 George Johnstone was the Aberdeen Goalkeeper in the first two Scottish Cup finals in which the club took part. Here he is fisting the ball away in a match against Rangers just after the war.

pitchforked at once into the Aberdeen team which played in the Empire Exhibition Tournament in 1938. In one of the strangest stories in Scottish footballing history he would still be an Aberdeen player when the next great Anglo-Scottish tournament, the Coronation Cup, came round in 1953. This was a record only equalled by Joe Mercer, that of playing in both competitions, and he was an Arsenal player in 1953 whereas he had been an Everton one fifteen years before.

It was perhaps because footballers like Hamilton and Baird had experienced extremely active service and seen friends and comrades die that they were such attractive players. Each had lost at a conservative estimate six years from the already short working life of a professional footballer. In exchange they had learned discipline and neatness, an unfailing appreciation of what was important in life and what was not, and a determination to enjoy the remainder of their careers in an essentially responsible way. In so doing, they would give incalculable joy to many thousands of people.

There were other new names. Two huge men in every sense were Joe McLaughlin, a Fifer possessed of a venomous shot who had suffered from being with Celtic during their lackadaisical war-time days, and Tony Harris, "Bomber" Harris as he was inevitably known in his time at Queen's Park. Harris had the broadest shoulders ever seen on a human being. They were, in the immortal words of Neil Munro's Para Handy, "like two fishboxes". This breadth did not prevent him being very speedy and he had played for Scotland at centre-forward in a war-time international at Hampden while still with Queen's Park. Aberdeen would use him first as a winger and then, as he moved into footballing middle-age, as an aggressive wing-half. The little South African, Stanley Williams, an acquisition from the ill-starred 1937 tour, had spent the war south of Aberdeen but had returned to show that he had lost none of his real ability to link a line. Willie Waddell to Pittodrie men did not mean the Rangers and Scotland winger but a young half-back who had arrived from the big city to the south in tandem with Archie Baird. The other South African, Billy Strauss, had gone and in his stead came Billy McCall, a Blantyre Victoria player, but the Dons could just as easily have whistled outside the gates of another dozen Lanarkshire mining villages.

It is difficult to envisage, in the materialistic and well-doing 90s, how hard things were almost fifty years ago. Difficult, but not impossible. Licences were required for almost everything, football strips, team buses, supporters' buses, building repairs. The railways had been battered almost to a standstill by six years of war, and to find a buffet car was a considerable achievement. Even when found it would have precious little to sell. The late winter of 1947 had been one of the worst in living memory, the snow came late but it came in feet rather than inches and as late as mid-March, some hundreds of English supporters who had come north for the Inter-League match at Hampden were marooned in a train near Carlisle for the better part of two days.

To add to the general misery there had been unrest in the mines and coal production had fallen. There were power cuts and the use of neon lighting was prohibited, while motoring for pleasure was of course out of the question.

The particular footballing complication was the need to avoid mid-week matches in the afternoons with the attendant high risk of absenteeism at a time when the major governmental slogan was "Export or Die!" Nor were matters helped by the insistence of both the S.F.A. and the Scottish League that the League Cup and Scottish Cup competitions should be played off almost simultaneously at a time of year when the weather was at its unrelenting worst. And, as the final factor in this equation, Aberdeen were in the worst fixtures plight of all because they would reach the final of both competitions.

The Dons' passage to the final of the Scottish Cup had been eventful enough, in all conscience. Drawn in the first round against Partick Thistle at Pittodrie, the sides were on a par at 1-1 with only a few minutes to separate Aberdeen from a dangerous and unwanted trip to Firhill for a replay. A speculative lob cum shot cum cross from the halfway line ended in the Partick Thistle net and the general astonishment at the sight of this bizarre goal was compounded when it was realised that the scorer was the Old Man of the side, Willie Cooper. Goals from him were rather less frequent in occurrence than the appearance of Halley's Comet, but as Shakespeare says, "when they seldom come, they wished-for come", and in 20 years with the club the big full-back was never to make a more telling contribution. The second round was easy with Ayr United making little or no resistance. Both Harris and Hamilton had hat-tricks in the 8-0 win at Pittodrie. There was a real threat to further progress when Morton succeeded where Partick Thistle had failed and did get a 1-1 draw at Pittodrie, but in a tight replay at Cappielow, goals by McCall and Hamilton enabled Aberdeen to squeeze through 2-1.

By now, the fixture backlog was assuming nightmare proportions and the decree went out that there could be no allocation of mid-week dates for cup-tie replays, they would have to be played to a finish. To a finish meant literally that, as Aberdeen were to discover at Dens Park where the sides were level after extra time, goals by Ewen for Dundee and Williams for Aberdeen cancelling each other out. It took a further ten minutes before Stan Williams got the goal which brought an immediate blast from the referee. And Aberdeen had got off lightly for at the same stage it had taken Hibernian no less than 142 minutes to dispose of Motherwell, at the end of which time the players were moving wearily around like the participants in the marathon dances which were so popular in the 1920s and 1930s.

On then to the semi-final, against unexpected opponents, Arbroath at Dens Park, and the fear that particularly marks semi-finals, the more so when the opposition is from a lower stratum of football. So congested was the football calendar by this time that Aberdeen were playing their semi-final on the same day that the England v. Scotland match was taking place at Wembley.

In the event, Aberdeen, wearing Arsenal-type jerseys for the day as their normal all-red jerseys clashed with the maroon of Arbroath, won comfortably enough, thanks to a brace of goals from the ebullient Williams. He was incidentally not the only South African to score for Aberdeen in their Cup run that year, Botha scoring one of the eight goals conceded by the luckless Ayr United. The Dons' semi-final win was turned almost to ashes by an injury to Willie Cooper who severely pulled a thigh muscle. The knock was aggravated by the fact that in those pre-substitute days he was compelled to hirple for some little time on the right wing, rather than have his team play a man short. "Even if he can do nothing it takes a man to mark him" was the philosophy of those rugged days. As the veteran limped from the field his joy at his side's being back at Hampden was diluted by the fact that the final was to take place only seven days later

31

and there was no possibility that he would have healed in that brief time. It was like General Wolfe or General Moore being killed in the moment of victory. The iron rule in those days for Scottish Cup medals was no medals for anyone but the eleven players. Twenty years of striving, and Willie Cooper would not even have a shot at a winner's medal.

That was bad enough. What was worse was that what he must now consider as his swan-song at Hampden had been a complete, though not a personal, disaster. A fortnight beforehand in the final of the League Cup, Rangers had exacted a powerful revenge for their 3-2 defeat of the previous year. On a day of driving wind and rain, Aberdeen had elected to face "the elements" as they were invariably called in sports reports, had miscalculated badly, lost three quick goals and the match was lost before it had properly begun. What a way to bow out!

Willie Cooper was of course with the party which went south to Glasgow for the final, this time the choice of accommodation was Largs. Even good hotels had still to contend with food rationing, another Coronation would come and go before we finally got rid of that. It was an austerity final for an austerity age and the 82,000 crowd contained not only many servicemen in uniform but many of their predecessors, immediately recognisable in demob suits and still more so in demob hats. The opponents were Hibernian, who were beyond a doubt the most attractive team in post-war Scotland and a side worthy of detailed analysis.

There were some possibly naïve notions going about. The *Press and Journal* commenting on the amount of national good will towards the Reds noted "All the way south the Dons popularity was evident from the V signs which came from railway workers along the line side". As George Gershwin's great character Sporting Life sings in *Porgy and Bess*, "It ain't necessarily so".

In the eight years which followed the Second World War, Hibernian were League champions three times, an unheard-of level of consistency for a team which did not belong to the Old Firm. They had the unenviable distinction of being regarded as half a team, since a couple of years after this particular final, everyone could reel off the names of their forward line, the Famous Five of Smith, Johnstone, Reilly, Turnbull, Ormond, while very few in numbers were those who could do the same for the defence. An Edinburgh evening paper carried this depreciation to extremes by showing a picture of the forward line and, above them, the defence cut off from the waist up.

On this bright and rather windy day of April 19, 1947, the following were the men clad in red and opposed by those in green and white.

ABERDEEN: Johnstone; McKenna, Taylor, McLaughlin, Dunlop, Waddell, Harris, Hamilton, Williams, Baird, McCall.

HIBERNIAN: Kerr; Govan, Shaw, Howie, Aird, Kean, Smith, Finnegan, Cuthbertson, Turnbull, Ormond.

Aberdeen manager, Dave Halliday, had dealt with the unavailability of Cooper by drafting in Pat McKenna to right back and George Taylor completed an entirely new full back division. With McLaughlin and Waddell occupying the wing-half berths, there would be a deal of adjustment to do.

Hibernian would take a lot of beating. In goal was Jimmy Kerr who, but for the war, might well have played for Scotland, and the full-back partnership of Govan and Shaw was more creative than the conventions of the time allowed most defenders to be. However statistically improbable, Davie Shaw was one of two Hibernian players that day who would go on to manage Aberdeen. Aird was a sound if dour centre-half while Sammy Kean had had the priceless experience of playing for two seasons during the war with such as Matt Busby, Bobby Baxter and Bob Hardisty of Middlesbrough and it should be said that no club had turned the war to greater advantage than Hibernian. They entered it a struggling relegation-haunted club and emerged from it as a power in the land.

The forward line had not escaped critical comment from Hibernian supporters. None of this was directed at right-winger, Gordon Smith, a player who to an unequalled degree married power with artistry. A Martian, watching Smith in the simple act of crossing a ball, would have known that he was in the presence of greatness. Smith would go on to achieve the greatest single individual feat in the history of Scottish League football, three championship medals with three separate clubs, Hibernian, Heart of Midlothian and Dundee.

At inside-right, Willie Finnegan was nearer the end of his career than the beginning but still a skilful, scheming forward who would need watching. The position which had caused heated debate in the East End of Edinburgh was centre-forward and the choice for it of John Cuthbertson, a lanky fellow with a nose for a chance but something lacking in the subtlety which had been a trade-mark of post-war Hibernian sides. The line was completed by two men who would certainly make their mark. Eddie Turnbull, the powerhouse of the forward line, would not only eventually manage Aberdeen, but win a Scottish Cup for them, while Willie Ormond, an outside-left whose skill was matched only by his physical courage, would eventually show as manager of St Johnstone and Scotland that his long years as a player had made him a very good judge of one.

Scottish football is a small and charmed circle and inevitably paths will cross, but for all that it is intriguing that the referee who set the game in motion that day was Bobby Calder, who would later, as a scout, smuggle almost as many West of Scotland players north to Aberdeen as the underground railway in America sent runaway slaves to freedom. The Aberdeen supporters settled down, some of the older minds going back ten years perhaps, to 1937.

The start was orthodox enough. From the kick-off, Aberdeen got possession, the ball moved towards their own defence, George Taylor in the unaccustomed position at left-back tapped the ball back to George Johnstone so that the goalkeeper could get a feel of the new ball. A perfectly normal move, almost every game started thus, the Aberdeen support turned its collective head away to talk to its neighbour or to light a cigarette; in those unreconstructed days there was never a second when a pin-point of light on the terracings did not denote that someone was lighting a fag.

Their attention was dragged back by an exultant shout. George Johnstone had unaccountably dropped the simplest of pass-backs and John Cuthbertson following up — a more intellectual forward would not have done so — was suddenly presented with a gaping goalmouth. With the air of a man for whom Christmas had come eight months or so early, he rammed the ball over the line and the Dons were a goal down with a minute on the clock. "Cubby" had no more worries. He had done HIS job.

What had gone wrong? Was it a conjunction of the new ball slipping against a new jersey? The more knowledgeable on the terraces remembered how this had happened to Arsenal in a Cup final against Cardiff City so that whenever Arsenal now reached a Cup final, the keeper's jersey was washed before the game to eliminate the risk of any repetition. Was this what had happened to Aberdeen?

Perhaps, but it didn't much matter. The initial numbness wore off the Aberdeen support though the best they could do for immediate comfort was that it was better to lose such a goal in the first minute rather than with a minute to go. They were heartened too by the fact that the players themselves seemed to have shrugged off the loss of the goal and were taking the game to Hibernian.

For the next fifteen minutes, they hammered the Edinburgh side's goal. Jimmy Kerr made life even more miserable for George Johnstone by saving brilliantly from Williams and Hamilton. A rasping shot from Billy McCall was inches out, so too one from Frank Dunlop, up to reinforce his forwards. In a couple of fugitive raids by Hibs, Johnstone handled well enough to indicate that he had got back his composure. But Aberdeen badly needed a goal.

They waited quite a time for it, until the 36th minute. Then McLaughlin sent of all things a long header boring into the wind, Stan Williams side-flicked it to where he intuitively knew George Hamilton would be. Hamilton finished the move with that clinical precision which was his trade-mark and Aberdeen were level.

Before half-time, they were ahead because Stan Williams did the wrong thing which turned out to be the right thing. He took a leaf from John Cuthbertson's book and went off on a forlorn hope of running down a Tony Harris pass which everyone else had given up as a goal-kick. Just managing to keep it in play, he set off for goal down the bye-line. All orthodox teaching should have led him to use the cut-back to the screaming Archie Baird and George Hamilton. But Williams, always a thinking player, had noticed that Jimmy Kerr was perhaps a foot off his line, anticipating as well he might, the cut-back or cross. Williams thereupon poked the ball, at no great speed, between Kerr and the post for the second Aberdeen goal. A keeper should not be beaten at his near post, so runs one of the immutable wise saws of the game, but it would be hard to blame Kerr for having gone on percentages.

1947 ABERDEEN v. HIBERNIAN. BEATEN AT THE NEAR POST. Stan Williams (out of picture) spots goalkeeper Jimmy Kerr off his line and finds the net at the near post for the winner.

It was the kind of goal George Best would often score in later years which would lead Bobby Charlton to yell "George, over here! George, square the bloody ball! George, you selfish little bugger! George, what a wonderful goal!"

And that unorthodox goal was all that separated the teams at the very end. It should not have been, for early in the second half when Stan Williams wriggled clear of the Hibernian defence, he was fetched down in the box by Jimmy Kerr in desperation. As clear-cut a penalty kick as you would ever wish to see, and who more fitted to take it than the disciplined and composed George Hamilton? Push the ball wide of Jimmy Kerr and there was no way back for Hibernian from a 1-3 score line. You would have put the rent money on George scoring and you would have been wrong. It was not the first Scottish Cup final penalty to be missed, Rangers had done this in 1929 and again in 1935, but Jimmy Kerr's dive to his left to clutch Hamilton's shot was a fine save by any standards. The Dons should have coasted home, instead there was considerable anxiety every time the Hibs forwards broke towards the Aberdeen goal, knowing that one defensive error would send the match to a replay.

There was no such error and, as even the longest river winds wearily to the sea, so even the longest second-half, and it was all that, is eventually terminated by the referee's whistle. A sea of red scarves and hats — well, not a sea, football folks were much more soberly dressed in those days — a rivulet of red scarves and hats saluted the achievement of these eleven Dons.

And of course, of the twelfth Don. Willie Cooper had looked on with pride and joy as his captain, Frank Dunlop, received the Scottish Cup in the centre circle, primitive days when such a presentation could be made completely free of the threat of loutish intervention. At the same time he would have been less than human had he not reflected that he had played twenty years for the club and some would win medals who had scarcely played the same number of games. If however he imagined that he had been forgotten in the moment of victory, his team-mates and the supporters speedily rid him of that notion. Eventually and shyly he responded to the unappeasable demands that he should go out and take a bow.

There is a remarkable photograph of the skipper Frank Dunlop, Stan Williams and George Johnstone with the Scottish

Cup, secured at long last, grins on their faces, their old-fashioned woollen jerseys soaked in sweat. With them, with an even more outsize smile, is Willie Cooper and despite the fact that he is wearing sports jacket and flannels, the great physical power of the man comes through. To their eternal credit, the S.F.A. acceded to the request of Aberdeen Football Club that a special medal should be struck for W. Cooper and he went into retirement the following year as a happy and fulfilled player.

Of that Aberdeen side none would know what it was to win a medal again at Hampden, though Harris and Hamilton would be back and so too would George Johnstone in a League Cup final for Dunfermline Athletic, although that was not a match that would leave the big keeper with too many happy memories. It mattered not, the Cup had been won and Aberdeen now ranked in every sense with the big boys. The return journey north could begin, with cheering crowds in every village, Aberdeen's streets packed, the civic reception that in years to come could almost be pencilled in on the calendar but which was then so strange.

Among the crowd was veteran club official and director William Philip, associated with the club since its foundation and now able at last to get his hands on "the old pot". As the *Press and Journal* editorial neatly put it "a hope of 40 years has been realised". The reserve players were able to get a look at the trophy too for, with what would now seem terrible hard-heartedness, they had been sent to Ibrox on the Saturday afternoon to play a Second Eleven Cup semi-final against Rangers and did very well to keep their minds sufficiently concentrated to earn a 2-2 draw.

And in triumph, spare a thought for Hibernian. None of that famous forward line ever did win a Scottish Cup medal. The supporters who had protested furiously that in the course of that season of 1946-47 the guileful Arthur Milne had been transferred, so too the speedy if erratic Jock Weir, that Leslie Johnstone had been signed to replace them but had not been signed in time to play, and that these three were all considerable centre-forwards, should reflect that for all that, John Cuthbertson was the player who DID SCORE for Hibernian.

We can spare but a passing thought for the opposition. Our concern is with Aberdeen and at the second time of asking, and against the collar, they had taken the premier knock-out trophy back to Pittodrie. Tony Harris had an additional satisfaction to come. When in 1967 certain newspapers mentioned in passing that Celtic's Jim Craig was the first dentist to win a Scottish Cup medal, Tony knew with complete certainty that he was not.

1947 — WILLIE COOPER REMEMBERS

"I was delighted to get another chance at the Scottish Cup in 1947 because, as I said, I was sure that the war had ended my career.

War-time football in the North-East League was quite enjoyable, you had the chance to play with players you would not otherwise have met such as Stan Mortensen and Willie Lyon who had played against us in the Cup Final in 1937. Alex Dyer who came from Portsmouth (actually Plymouth Argyle — author) was also a good player.

Of course in war-time you had to have a full-time job and I went back to being an engineer, a marine engineer. We trained after five o'clock and even then only could do ball work in the light nights but playing kept you fairly fit.

In 1947, I remember of course scoring the winner against Partick Thistle with a few minutes to go. I didn't score very many goals, about 5 in all my years at Pittodrie although in the 30s I scored twice in quick succession against Clyde and Cowdenbeath. I think I remember that because I scored so few goals! I was never a penalty taker.

The Dundee match was very hard because we had been told that we were out on the pitch until someone scored the winner so we were very glad when Stan Williams scored the winner after 130 minutes, in extra extra time as you might say. In the semi-final against Arbroath, I knew right away that my leg had gone and that I'd no chance of making the final. It wouldn't have made any difference if we had been allowed substitutes in those days, I still would have had no chance of being ready in a week.

I always thought that Paddy Travers was the better manager but maybe that's because I believed Dave Halliday wanted me out of the side and Andy Cowie, who had started at right-half, to take over from me at right-back. I did manage to hang on to my position until the time came for me to leave Pittodrie. I remember the 1947 Final well although I was never a good watcher. When George Johnstone dropped the ball in the first minute and Hibernian scored we thought "Oh dear, that is it already".

It was wonderful to go out to the cheers of the crowd at the end and I was very pleased that the S.F.A. had agreed to award me a medal but of course that can never be the same thing as winning one for actually taking part in the game. I did another season or so and when I left I had been at Pittodrie for 21 years. I was keen to carry on playing but I knew my first division days were over. I went up to the Highland League for a season with Huntly and would you believe it, I won a cup medal with them in my one and only season there!"

CHAPTER THREE

1953 v. RANGERS

UNCROWNED AT THE CORONATION

Once again it was a Coronation year and once again Aberdeen had reached the Scottish Cup Final. It had taken eight years for things to revert to normal after the war but at long last this had happened. The last vestiges of food rationing were going; a man could take his car out for a pleasure run without being accused of being a traitor to the nation, and for the first time in fourteen years, supplies of newsprint exceeded demand. There would therefore be no shortage of column inches to describe the Dons' success or failure at Hampden.

For the first time also they would meet Rangers in the last stage. The Ibrox side were the antithesis of Aberdeen's previous Scottish Cup Final opponents, Hibernian. They relied basically on a dour and competent defence and the ability to score in breakaways. An interesting sidelight is that although Rangers won the League with great frequency they top-scored comparatively seldom in that competition. Two of their most renowned forwards, Willie Thornton and Willie Waddell, were at the very end of their distinguished careers, Thornton indeed no longer laid claim to a first-team place.

Manager David Halliday, who had joined Aberdeen from the cumbrously-named Yeovil and Petters United in 1938, was confident that Rangers could be beaten, an opinion shared by several Press men. It was true that on the day Aberdeen supporters would be outnumbered by between three and four to one, that was inevitable in those days of six figure attendances. It was also true that the Rangers support was fiercely implacable, creating a menacing noise which could and did deter all but the strongest referees. The official chosen for this final was Jack Mowat of Burnside so that was at least one difficulty removed. He would referee as he saw it.

It was the club's Golden Jubilee year and therefore especially fitting that the oldest trophy should come north to Pittodrie. The crowning of a young Queen had created a curiously hopeful atmosphere, later there would be an Anglo-Scottish tournament, the Coronation Cup, and Aberdeen had been invited to take part in it as one of the country's leading clubs.

The passage to the field had been the not unusual mixture of brilliance and stumbling. Loss of concentration and two goals in the last six minutes let Motherwell gain an unlikely 5-5 draw at Pittodrie after St Mirren had been set aside. The Fir Park team were incredibly then thrashed 6-1 in the replay. To dispose of Hibernian was a considerable feat in the early 1950s even although another replay was required. What was more worrying was that it had taken two games to subdue a very ordinary Third Lanark side at the semi-final stage. The supporters could justifiably maintain that there had been no soft options in the draw, four first-division sides met, four first-division sides accounted for.

The one link with pre-war Aberdonian football, George Hamilton, demonstrated that the years had touched him but lightly when he scored the two goals that did for Hibernian in the replay at Pittodrie and in the semi-final replay against Third Lanark it was Harry Yorston who was on the mark twice after Thirds had gone ahead. The team did not lack determination nor the ability to come from behind.

There were still almost as many special trains as there had been in 1937, 14 as against 17. There were 140 buses, hundreds of cars as the pre-war models were taken down from the blocks in dusty garages where they had long reposed and, a sign of coming fashions, a couple of aeroplane flights from what had been the old R.A.F. station at Dyce. At the other end of the velocity scale were a handful of cyclists who left Aberdeen late in the afternoon and hoped, greatly daring, to be in Glasgow sometime the following morning. At least they missed the attentions of the Students Charities Week monster, Marilyn, which was wheeled to the station so that its owners could fleece the departing fans in a worthwhile cause. No matter the mode of transport selected by each individual fan, a win at Hampden would finally redeem a less than impressive season of League football in which 30 games had brought a mere 27 points, and eleventh place.

Hampden was little short of a capacity crowd as the players lined up in the centre circle before 135,000 expectant spectators.

ABERDEEN: Martin; Mitchell, Shaw, Harris, Young, Allister, Rodger, Yorston, Buckley, Hamilton, Hather.

RANGERS: Niven; Young, Little, McColl, Stanners, Pryde, Waddell, Grierson, Paton, Prentice, Hubbard.

On the Aberdeen side, Freddie Martin provides the rarest of cases, that of a player signed by a senior club as an inside-forward who became an international goalkeeper and played in the World Cup at that. In parenthesis, even more unlikely perhaps was the fact that one of his almost-immediate successors, Bobby Clark, was signed as a goalkeeper from Queen's Park but played at least one full game as an outfield player.

At right back was Jimmy Mitchell, a former Queen's Parker at a time when there was a fairly constant stream of players from Hampden to Pittodrie. Tony Harris, Alan Boyd and goalkeeper John Curran are others who came to mind. Mitchell had arrived by an indirect route, having been a Morton stalwart for some seasons and a member of their losing Final side in 1948. He therefore knew what it was like to see a Light Blue presentation. His partner Davie Shaw had also surmounted every Cup hurdle bar one and hoped that this time with Aberdeen he would lift the trophy as a team mate and not as the opponent he had been back in 1947.

In the autumn of his football days Tony Harris had stepped back to right-half where his colleagues were Alec Young, not noticeably much taller than Eddie Falloon but with the same gritty command of the air, and Jack Allister. The forward line had the recognised mix of two pacy wingers, Ian Rodger and the Englishman from the North-East, Jackie Hather,

45

two finishers in Harry Yorston and Paddy Buckley, secured from St Johnstone although his career might well have started and ended with Everton, and the indestructible, thoughtful George Hamilton.

The interesting thing about the Rangers team is to reflect on who was NOT playing. It has to be said that at first glance it was one of the most unlikely and anonymous Rangers sides ever to have taken part in a Scottish Cup final. George Niven was essentially a brave goalkeeper, small for that position but a thorough professional who had not allowed his five year apprenticeship in the reserves at Ibrox either to sour him or to take the edge off his technique and reflexes.

George Young had grown from the lanky stringbean of 1941 into a footballing giant in every sense. Now of considerable girth he could appear ponderous and slow, but still those great long legs came flicking out to dispossess the forward who thought all too optimistically that he had evaded the big defender. Young's immediate opponent also had the comforting knowledge that he would be played hard but scrupulously fairly. Few top defenders who played so long can so seldom have committed a deliberate foul.

At left-back was the speedy Johnny Little, who had started his career with Queen's Park with notions of being a centre-forward. He would replace Sammy Cox who had been injured at Wembley a few days before, after starring in a 2-2 draw against England. Little had it for pace but the fierce, driving tackling of Cox might well be missed. At right-half was Ian McColl, also on his original home ground, renowned for the skill with which he could pull the hip-high ball from the air, control it and send it in its intended direction. An unfamiliar name would take the centre-half spot, Duncan Stanners, who made little impact at Ibrox but now found himself part of the greatest single occasion in Scottish football. He was there because Willie Woodburn, a beautifully elegant pivot but of uncertain reaction where football was concerned, had got himself sent off in a spectacularly evil-tempered match against Clyde and was consequently under suspension.

The left-half position was filled by John Prentice and therefore curiously the Rangers line-up contained two future Scotland managers, Ian McColl being the other. On the right wing was Willie Waddell, having his last Cup Final canter, having also lost a yard or so in speed but his ability to shoot with the inside foot as Stan Williams had done in 1947 rendered him a constant danger. Another ex-Queen's Parker was Derek Grierson, this was at a time when Rangers not infrequently signed half a Queen's Park side — Cox had also been a Spider and Woodburn a trialist there — and he was especially dangerous for his quick darts through the centre and his unexpected strength on the ball. Willie Paton and John Prentice were tall, powerful forwards in the mould traditionally favoured by Rangers who took some persuading that a good little 'un was as useful as a good big 'un and the South African connection was unexpectedly continued in the presence of Johnny Hubbard at outside-left. This waif-like figure had convinced initially doubtful Rangers officials that he was as good as any six-footer. Perhaps the most accomplished penalty taker of all time in Scottish football — the author is inclined to attribute this to the fact that Johnny frequently practised against him while in the same R.A.F. side — every Dons supporter knew that any foul conceded in the penalty area would result in a trip for Fred Martin to the back of Hampden's capacious nets.

The crowd addressed itself to the business of the day, none more so than the officials of Newburgh Juniors since the little Fife club found itself in the unprecedented position of providing not one but two players for a Scottish Cup final, Rodger on the Aberdeen side and Pryde appearing for Rangers.

The Aberdeen contingent was understandably optimistic. You had to fancy the Dons, didn't you, what with no Cox, no Woodburn and no Billy Simpson, who had been ordered off in the same torrid match as his centre-half? You had to fancy them, certainly, but you had to remember that Rangers' great reputation had not been won solely by fortunate breaks or debatable decisions. Relishing their unwonted role as underdogs, they went ahead in eight minutes with a goal from John Prentice. This was grievous indeed but Aberdeen had fought back before in this year's Cup campaign, could they do it now when it mattered crucially?

The stars in their courses seemed to be with the Northerners a few minutes later when goalkeeper George Niven plunged bravely at the feet of an Aberdeen forward and did not get up. Anxious team-mates summoned a stretcher and he was carried to the pavilion, blood pouring from an ear. George

1953 THE MOMENT BEFORE. Paddy Buckley eludes Rangers Johnny Little and is stopped by a death or glory dive by keeper George Niven.

Young somehow or other squeezed his enormous frame into the medium-small jersey worn by the luckless keeper. The ten men found a little extra as ten men often do. Sides struggling a man short are the stuff of footballing legend. So mighty are the feats attributed to them, and still more to nine-men garrisons, that one can only wonder that managers still retain the preference to start matches with the original eleven. The 1953 final was no different. George Young handled confidently enough — especially when a goalkeeper's jersey that was a better fit was fetched out — but in truth he was not asked to stop anything that a reasonably agile Girl Guide could not have saved. Whether from a misplaced sense of chivalry or from the paralysis of will that sometimes afflicts a team facing depleted opponents, Young was allowed to survive an easy passage when he should have been made to handle at every opportunity.

There was no change to the score when the teams went in at half-time, Rangers supporters the more anxious of the two despite the fact that they were ahead. As the players came out again for the second half, there was a mighty roar from the Rangers end for there was the ashen-faced figure of George Niven, head swathed in a towel, blood still seeping through it but determined to take his place in goal. It was courage of the highest order and Aberdeen fans were generous enough to recognise it, as Rangers trainer Jimmy Smith and an ambulanceman took up precautionary post behind Niven's goal.

Aberdeen had the better of the second half though desperation tinged their efforts as time slid away. Twice they might have had penalty kicks, twice Jack Mowat played advantage, twice the palpable chances were spurned. When it seemed as if this makeshift Iron Curtain defence would record yet another notable triumph, the red shirts managed the equaliser. Yorston found Hather on the left — curiously Cyril Horne of the *Glasgow Herald* was to criticise the Aberdeen left flank for lack of pace — the Englishman crossed and Yorston made ground to deliver a header which even at his fittest George Niven could not have saved.

The vast Rangers support were silenced but not stunned. They knew, and believed, that conventional Scottish football wisdom said that you got one chance and one chance only at a Scottish Cup final against either member of the Old Firm. Rangers had not lost a replay since they started winning

1953 COME ON THE TEN MEN. Niven is led off suffering from a severe ear injury. Here he is being assisted by Rangers trainers Jimmy Smith and Joe Craven. George Young is about to pull on the keeper's jersey while an anxious Willie Waddell holds the sponge.

Scottish Cups again in 1928. Moreover, their team was bound to be stronger, and the more pernickety of their supporters would have pointed out that they had not lost a Cup Final replay since 1905, if you wanted to be pedantic about it.

The Press was divided, some writers attributing the failure of Aberdeen to win to sheer back luck, but Alan Breck of the *Evening Times* would have none of that. "It was not" he said, "so much a case of sheer bad luck as of an Aberdeen team which did not have the skill to finish off their outfield excellence".

So it was a replay, never good news for Aberdeen. It was difficult for their supporters to get down to Glasgow, especially for those of them who lived furth of the town itself. It was just as difficult, even for those who managed to make the second trip, to screw themselves up to a similar pitch of excitement, there is almost always a dead hand on replayed finals.

The main question was, what would Rangers do in the matter of team selection. Would George Niven be fit to play? He was, with a form of scrum-cap covering the gashed ear which had required four stitches from the doctor on the spot. Would Sammy Cox be ready? He would not, a bad muscle strain would take a long time to respond. Woodburn would come back at centre-half, that could be taken for granted and he had to be a better bet than the plucky but inexperienced Stanners. No doubt to his considerable chagrin, John Prentice found that the goal which he had scored on the Saturday was not sufficient to keep him in the Light Blues' side and his place was taken by Billy Simpson, fit and available again after suspension.

And, as any Aberdeen supporter could have told you he would, Simpson scored the winner, the only goal, after 41 minutes, a time when to lose a goal is like a severe blow to the solar plexus. Yet again Aberdeen had most of the play and little good it did them. Hather struck the bar, sent a shot screaming past and Young scraped a deflected Yorston shot off the line. The towering Rangers captain was later booked — a comparatively rare occurrence then in a Cup final — for attempting to referee; some Aberdeen supporters might just be able to identify a similar trait in one of their modern star players!

It was a long way back north, it always is after a defeat but the miles felt especially leaden to the Aberdeen supporters among the 113,000 crowd because of the sense that this had

1953 THE EQUALISER AT LAST. George Niven came back to the Rangers goal and performed heroically but could do nothing to stop this fine header from Harry Yorston which earned the Dons a replay.

been a priceless opportunity tossed away. The Cup had been lost on the Saturday, however, not the Wednesday and those supporters waiting for very late trains and looking for a cinema to while away the hours might have seen barbed metaphors leaping from almost every poster outside every picture house. *The Cruel Sea* — that could only be the mass of blue scarves waving exultantly as George Young hoisted the Cup aloft. The *Crimson Pirate* — surely the bloodstained and bespattered George Niven who had never won a Cup medal before but was determined he'd get one as he had literally sweated blood for it. And *Botany Bay* — that could only refer to the transports of frustration that Pittodrie followers were undergoing.

"Be it so, by St Mary there's comfort in store." So runs the Gaelic poem and if Aberdeen in their fifty years, a jubilee frequently referred to during their pre-match stay at Gleneagles, had never succeeded in defeating Rangers in a Scottish Cup-tie the time was fast approaching when all the past disappointments and failures would be swept aside in one of the most outstanding days in the club's long history.

Before that day was reached some famous names would have departed Pittodrie. There can seldom have been a more distinguished free transfer list for Tommy Pearson of the hypnotic double shuffle was going. So too was Archie Baird, who had shrugged off three years as a prisoner of war to return to play at the highest level with club and country. Chris Anderson's playing days were over but, useful wing-half though he had been, it was as an official that he was destined to make by far his greatest contribution to the prosperity of the Dons. Finally, Ernie Ewan had played his last game in a red jersey. It was time to make a new beginning, the last of the pre-war men were striding into retirement.

1953 — GEORGE HAMILTON REMEMBERS

The Cup Final against Rangers in 1953 was my second with Aberdeen. I had already won a medal against Hibernian in 1947 and even by that time I was 29 years old. The war hadn't been as damaging to me as I had thought because in the Central Mediterranean Forces side I played with such great players as Tom Finney of Preston North End, Willie Thornton of Rangers, our own Billy Strauss of Aberdeen and the great Stan Cullis of Wolves. A young player could only improve in company like that.

I remember that Hibs final because I played quite well but missed a penalty when we led 2-1. I knew that Jimmy Kerr, the Hibernian goalkeeper, was very left-handed and that he'd expect me to shoot to his right. I thought I'd fox him and hit the ball to his left side, the stronger side, but he out-guessed me and made a good save. For the rest of the match, I was terrified that Hibs would equalise in one of their attacks and I would have cost Aberdeen the Scottish Cup. But we held on to win and came home to a great reception in pouring rain. I think I missed the penalty because there was a considerable hold-up while Stan Williams was treated for injury. He had been brought down by Jimmy Kerr in the area and perhaps that gave me too much time to think. A penalty kick is a simple matter of making up your mind where you want it to go and I second-guessed.

The goal I scored was a good one - a pass from Archie Baird to Billy McColl, a good cross and a head-flick from me and that was the equaliser. (NB: This account is quite different from contemporary newspaper descriptions of this goal.) So as I say I already had a medal when we went back in 1953. We should have beaten Rangers that day. They were without Cox, Woodburn and Simpson, a big bite out of their team. We were unaccountably edgy, even when George Niven went off we hardly had a decent shot at George Young who of course filled the goal anyway! In the end we were lucky to get a late draw although Harry Yorston's goal was a great effort.

We played better in the replay although we lost 1-0. We had some great characters in the team, notably Tony Harris who was a fine player, very powerful and speedy for such a burly man. That didn't always save him from our own supporters. There was one game at Pittodrie when Tony was badly off-form. An announcement was made at half-time that half a railway ticket had been found and someone in the stand immediately shouted "Give it to Harris".

The replay against Rangers was difficult, you had to gear yourself up for another big match. I don't like the modern way of penalties very much but perhaps it is better than a replay. I thought at the time that play to a finish would have been better and of course we did that once during the 1947 run, against Dundee it was.

We were much better in the second game but still lost. Rangers were a very dour and battling side, George Young was a difficult opponent but I thought Willie Woodburn was the real footballer in the defence. I came away from Hampden that year thinking "Well, that's it as far as Scottish Cups go" but of course I was back playing in a final the very next season. Those of us who had been in the war were very conscious that in a sense our post-war football was a bonus. Maybe that is why we enjoyed it so much.

CHAPTER FOUR

1954 v. CELTIC

BEWARE THE MAKESHIFT CENTRE-FORWARD

With hindsight, it seems incredible that Aberdeen did not win the Scottish Cup in 1954. If ever a side had done all the hard work on the road to the final, it was the Aberdeen team of that year. On their way to Hampden, they had defeated Hibernian 3-1 at Easter Road, Hearts 3-0 at Pittodrie and Rangers for the first time ever in a Scottish Cup tie by the unbelievable margin of 6-0, all the frustrations of the previous half-century suddenly being unleashed.

The game with Hearts at the quarter-final stage in 1954 established a Pittodrie ground record of 45,061 and sent the author chasing to the reference books thinking that this must be an error and that this record had in fact been set the following year when the two clubs met at the same stage in a replay. The writer favoured 1955 because, then stationed at R.A.F. Edzell, he had got the afternoon off and with two colleagues arrived at the Beach End with fifteen minutes to go before kick-off, gaining admission just before the gates clanged shut. The effort was wasted as for the next two hours we clung precariously to the top step of the terracing at that end, occasionally launching ourselves high into the air to ascertain that there was some green grass down there and the occasional maroon jersey. The record books were right, however, there were 2,000 or so less at the 1955 replay so conditions the year before must have beggared description. It enabled one to relate perfectly to the anonymous Aberdonian at Hampden in 1937.

The 1954 Cup run had begun with a pleasant away stroll against the "Dingers" or Duns, to give the little East of Scotland side its Sunday name. A professional club was in one sense bound to regard an eight goal margin as a waste of time but could perhaps register Brownie points for missionary work. If that was an accommodating draw from the imp of the ballot box (it was still being so described), that same sprite decided that henceforth Aberdeen would progress by the sweat of their brow. Hibernian, Hearts, Rangers.

Inevitably, back at Hampden for the second year running, there were similarities in team selection (although late injury made for more changes than might have been expected) and in league performance. Aberdeen would startle Scottish football by winning the League in 1955 but it was a surprise in that their performances in the two previous seasons had been lacklustre, eleventh of sixteen in 1953, ninth of sixteen in 1954.

One of football's abidingly intriguing mysteries is the appearance of the shooting star, who does something marvellous and very transient before disappearing from human ken. Aberdeen's man of the semi-final was a Glaswegian and he wore a skull-cap of sorts as George Niven had done the year before. Joe O'Neil, up from the Glasgow Junior club, Bridgeton Waverley, was scarcely more than a fringe player and the decision to field him against Rangers smacked of the foolhardy as he had sustained a depressed fracture of the skull only weeks before. This was to be his lovely day, however, and before a crowd which would have more than graced the final itself, 110,000 were there, he himself scored three and would have had four in all probability had he not been chopped in the penalty area. It made no odds, where O'Neil might have scored, Allister did with the given penalty. For the record, not that it mattered by then to the delirious Dons fans, Graham Leggat and Paddy Buckley got the remaining two goals. Long before the finish the Rangers fans had vanished over the rim of the vast Hampden terracing like Indians leaving the scene in a Western.

The loyalty even of the follow-follow boys had its

limits, a fact commented upon by the sports writers in attendance at the match. Alan Breck of the *Evening Times* delivered this shaft:

"The flag-wavers had departed long since. One suspected that they could not take it."

One not only suspected it, one knew it for certain. There had been signs that the Rangers defence was not the impregnable fortress of old, shortly beforehand it had yielded four goals at Falkirk. The Ibrox side too were once again unlucky against Aberdeen in the way of injury. Their dashing goalkeeper, Bobby Brown, sustained an injury as early as the second minute which markedly reduced his effectiveness and full back Johnny Little was compelled to play part of the match at outside-left. At a time when the outcome was still doubtful, Rangers twice struck the crossbar, Prentice and Simpson being the players who came within inches of success.

But injury was part and parcel of cup-tie football in those pre-substitute days. What was new was the chilling efficiency with which the Aberdeen forwards exploited the slightest suggestion of weakness or hesitancy in the Rangers defence. That most elegant of writers, Cyril Horne of the *Glasgow Herald*, whose dislike of the crowd trouble which attended Rangers just occasionally led him to be over-severe in matches where they were involved, referred to the singing of "one of the more lugubrious of the Rangers dirges, *'There's not a team like the Glasgow Rangers'*, which contains the line *'Celtic know all about their troubles'*."

Horne went on to say "It is almost certainly true that Celtic will know all about their troubles when Aberdeen meet them". Certainly, for once in a way, Aberdeen were entitled to consider themselves as favourites even in a Scottish Cup final in which a member of the Old Firm was involved. The bookmakers, however, those consummate judges, could not separate the teams. Celtic had done little of note for the last ten years and would do very little for the next ten. They had not won the Scottish League since 1938 and what was more, had never looked remotely like doing so. They seemed to have settled for a comfortable middle of the table existence. Their Scottish Cup record was little better, one solitary post-war success against Motherwell in 1951.

And yet . . . and yet. They had picked this season 1953-54 to win the League championship, so for them the double was on. The previous summer, both Aberdeen and Celtic had found themselves invited to play against the pick of England in the Coronation Cup. Celtic were not there on current playing ability but on sentiment and as guaranteed ground-fillers. This back door mode of entry did not prevent their winning the competition and disposing of Arsenal and Manchester United in the by-going. The commitment of English clubs to such tournaments was always a shade suspect but no top-rank team deliberately courts public humiliation at the hands of an opponent.

Once again, the Aberdeen followers streamed south, nearly a hundred of them in three thirty-two seater planes. Britain's roads were still narrow and quiet, one went to the Hampden finals from Aberdeen by train. The leaving time had got a little earlier with the years, if you were keen enough you could depart from Aberdeen at 2.45 a.m. and be in Glasgow by 6.30 to get ahead of the neighbours. The corridors were packed with standing supporters and a fine early morning in Glasgow gave promise of heat.

Immediately Fate was to deal a bad blow to the red legions. Joe O'Neil, who had been so instrumental in the semifinal win and who had so bravely come back from a serious head knock, was now side-lined because of a foot injury sustained, with a weary inevitability, against Rangers in a league match. He was able to derive some considerable consolation from the birth of his first child, a boy who might just go on to make a final someday himself. The choice of substitute can wait a moment for discussion as, before the teams kicked off, there was considerable misbehaviour from a section of the Celtic support during the playing of the National Anthem. The Celtic Board, aware that this was a possibility, had done their best to forestall trouble by asking those of their supporters who disapproved of the sentiments contained therein to maintain a dignified silence, but they could have saved their breath. Cyril Horne in the *Glasgow Herald* infuriatedly showed that on the matter of misbehaviour, he played no favourites:

"What the Aberdeen players, officials and supporters think of Glasgow must be easy to imagine. A fortnight ago they had the Union Jack thrust in their faces with an accompanying

barrage of allegedly patriotic noise and now they get the Tricol-
our and its comparable inanity."

When the farmyard imitations subsided and things got
under way, it could be seen that it was with the following
teams:

ABERDEEN: Martin; Mitchell, Caldwell, Allister,
Young, Glen, Leggat, Hamilton, Buckley, Clunie, Hather.

CELTIC: Bonnar; Haughney, Meechan, Evans, Stein,
Peacock, Higgins, Fernie, Fallon, Tully, Mochan.

The passage of one solitary year had entailed four changes
in an Aberdeen line-up that, with one significant exception,
looked to have the stronger forward line. Davie Caldwell came
in at left-back where Davie Shaw had been a twelvemonth
before. Tony Harris had gone so Allister moved to right
midfield (although the benighted souls did not then know the
term) and the artistic Archie Glen took up the left-half spot.
The fast and thrilling teenager, Graham Leggat, was handed
responsibility for the right wing but the choice of Joe O'Neil's
deputy raised a wheen of eyebrows.

The boots of the absent hero would be filled by the
young Jim Clunie, signed from Raith Rovers as a centre-half
only the previous December and with one solitary game for the
first team in that position. Jim Clunie was big and strong and
willing but it was asking an awful lot of a young laddie to play
him in so important a match and in such a foreign position. It
seemed as if manager Davie Halliday was taking the most
tremendous gamble.

It was a mark of Celtic's prolonged period of non-success
that as many as six of their players were appearing in their first
Scottish Cup final, Bonnar, Meechan, Stein, Higgins, Fernie and
Mochan. Still, it could not be forgotten that Bobby Evans was
a regular Scottish internationalist and Willie Fernie a spasmodic
one, Evans combative, fiery, ever driving forward, Fernie the
mazy dribbler who sometimes seemed to forget where he was
going and why, and there were no fewer than three men in the
side who had played for Northern Ireland, Bertie Peacock,
Charlie Tully and Sean Fallon. Tully was the great practical
joker of Scottish football, his cantrips far from universally
appreciated by opponents or for that matter, colleagues. He was
an intricate, close-working ball player with a love of the

outrageous (getting possession from a throw-in by throwing the ball against the back of a retreating opponent) and unexpected. Any club would welcome the presence of Fernie OR Tully in a forward line but having both might prove to be something of a luxury.

Celtic had also caused groans with a forward selection. Sean Fallon was a resourceful, brave and accomplished full-back in the traditional mode, but was from time to time drafted up front when goals were in short supply. He was not a natural centre-forward, although as strongly-built as McGrory had been, and in that role he was rarely more than adequate. He had one great gift, however, and that was his thorough profession-alism. He probably had two, for allied to that was a complete personal unselfishness which would lead him to play and do his very best, wherever selected by his club.

The third Irishman, Bertie Peacock, was for years an automatic selection for his country and would in most people's eyes have been the natural captain. That office however was reserved for an even more remarkable man who, like some Old Testament prophet, had come out of the football desert that was South Wales. Jock Stein was never more than a middling to good First Division player (he described himself as very ordi-nary but he was perceptibly better than that). He was a great observer and possessed a real gift for captaincy, his contribution to leadership far exceeded the ability to distinguish heads from tails on a coin of the realm. In retrospect, this was to be a highly important match for his future managerial career. It helped to convince players that what you said was probably right when you could produce your own personal Cup and League medals. "What did you do in the war, Daddy?" "I won the double, son."

But the double was not won at three o'clock on that Saturday afternoon and at kick-off many fancied that the young, dynamic Leggat, the whippet, Buckley, and the Old Controller, George Hamilton, might have the last word on that particular afternoon.

They made a bright enough start, compelling the Celtic goalkeeper Johnny Bonner to show that lack of inches was offset by corresponding ability. Hamilton came close, so did Buckley. It was a first half that essentially belonged to the defences, however, nothing got past Stein at one end of the park and as little passed Young at the other. Interval reflections were that it might well require a return to Glasgow in mid-week if one were to be in at the death.

It did not work out like that for there were two quick second-half goals, although they did cancel each other out. Celtic took the lead in 51 minutes with what was harshly accredited as an own goal to Alex Young. The Celtic outside-left, Neil Mochan, fired a hard cross-cum-shot towards the goal and, although Fred Martin seemed set to receive it, the diversion took the ball beyond his reach. Young could well have been absolved from blame however, for this was a frequent ploy of "Smiler" Mochan. He had done the same thing in a Charity Cup final at Hampden in 1953 against Queen's Park and he would do the same again in the famous 7-1 defeat of Rangers in the League Cup final in 1957.

At all events, there were no post-mortems, no recriminations and in an incredible repeat of the 1937 Cup final scenario, Aberdeen were again on level terms against Celtic within a minute. An excellent goal it was too, with nothing of the chancy about it, Leggat supplying the pass to Buckley who, confronted with both Jock Stein and the goalkeeper, resisted the temptation to lash out but simply drew the keeper and stroked the ball into the untenanted goal.

Now perhaps the game could have been said to have turned Aberdeen's way, with Archie Glen driving on from wing-half, the outstanding player on the field that day. Celtic soaked up the pressure, almost 70 years of tradition coming to their rescue, and when the decider came, it went to the green and whites. Fernie set off on a corkscrew run down the right with an ambling gait which looked slow until one noticed the pursuing defender, arms pumping like pistons but still toiling in his wake. Fernie slipped past two defenders, looked up, saw Fallon bustling into position and laid the ball in his tracks. The standby centre-forward ran on and, despite the presence of two Aberdeen defenders on the goal-line, sent the ball to the back of the net.

It was a totally unremarkable goal in some ways, excluding the meander of Fernie, but the stand-in had done his job and the Aberdeen forward line, in which Clunie wrought courageously but was palpably out of place, could not find an equaliser. The whistle came with the single goal advantage for Celtic and the best Aberdeen could do was once again to win friends in adversity for what was described in the Press as a spontaneous display of gracefulness in defeat.

That final of 1954 has to go down as an opportunity sadly lost. George Hamilton would not see another Scottish Cup final but in a bizarre postscript to an honourable and successful career, he was selected for the Scottish party to take part in the World Cup in Switzerland in the later summer. Conscripted might have been a more appropriate word since, left to his own devices, George might well have preferred to have been playing golf over his beloved Edzell. He would have been employed just as usefully had he done so for, having been chosen, he played neither in the narrow defeat by Austria, nor in the massacre of the 7-0 rout by Uruguay.

Fred Martin did, and indeed for him it was not an option as Scotland set off with a squad of only 13 players so that had Martin been injured in the first match, an outfield player would have had to take over for the Uruguay game. It was an example of S.F.A. organisation at its absolute worst.

All that was in the immediate future. The dispirited fans trudged north, thwarted once again. Spirits were further depressed by a very bad car accident which resulted in the death of five of those supporters who had set out that day with such high hopes. It was some consolation, not too much in the short term, that the support was widely perceived by the media as being in general composed of more likeable people than that which followed their two great West of Scotland rivals. Cyril Horne in the *Herald* had the last word.

"Aberdeen have retired to the North, perhaps reflecting that the air up there is much cleaner and even without the Cup it is a better place."

That was all very well and in its way quite gratifying, but there were many of the returning fans who would have cheerfully foregone some of the praise if in return they could have seen the Scottish Cup hoisted aloft in Union Street for a second time. Failure to beat Rangers or Celtic in the ultimate stage was a psychological barrier which needed to be overcome soon. That day would come, but not yet awhile.

There was a chance of three consecutive appearances in 1955, but Aberdeen faltered with an apparently easy semi-final draw against Clyde. They lost after a replay but Clyde showed that it was the year of the underdog by themselves defeating

Celtic in the final after two games, the repeated Celtic experiment of putting Fallon once more in the forward line being this time unsuccessful. It was a time of bizarre experimentation for Celtic in important matches. In 1956, they would produce right-back Mike Haughney out of the blue — if that phrase can be used in a Celtic connection — against Hearts, at centre forward with a striking lack of success.

For, as the experiment with Jim Clunie shows, moving players forward seldom works despite Sean Fallon's goal. Joe O'Neil's absence was perhaps fatally damaging and even sadder was the fact that he would soon drift away from Pittodrie. Still, there was the nucleus of a good side in Glen, Leggat and Buckley. And next year, like tomorrow, was another day.

If further solace were needed there was the splendid news that George Hamilton had again been honoured by his country. Musing that it was odd that Scotland should need to cap a 36 year old, the *Press and Journal* nevertheless asked the rhetorical question "Where is there a better?" and went on to pay this graceful tribute: "No more modest or gentlemanly player and certainly none more skilful has ever won the affection of the Pittodrie football public."

1954 ABERDEEN v. CELTIC. Jock Stein who would later become more famous as a manager did have one highly successful year in 1954. Here he is seen on his way to a League and Cup double, as he passes back to John Bonnar.

1954 — GEORGE HAMILTON REMEMBERS

It's strange but I remember the semi-final in 1954 much more clearly than the final. That was the game in which we beat Rangers 6-0, quite ironical for me because coming from Irvine I had been very much a Rangers supporter as a lad. In fact I got the length of a trial at Ibrox. I played for the second team against Galston in the old Alliance league but nothing came of it although I eventually got my wish to wear a Rangers jersey when I guested for them a few times in the early days of the war.

Nobody, but nobody, beat Rangers 6-0 in those days. It was an unbelievable match for us, we could do nothing wrong. I can only compare it to those days when you go out on the golf course and begin to hole putts from all distances and angles until you feel that if you closed your eyes while putting the ball would still go into the hole. Joe O'Neil had a field day, he scored three goals and we really did play excellent football.

We had a very good side and Freddie Martin was a fine goalkeeper. He would always play outfield in training sessions and he was a good player, it wasn't by any means a keeper just having a joke. He had been signed of course as an inside-forward. I myself had been brought to Pittodrie by Dave Halliday as a replacement for the famous Willie Mills, a heavy responsibility for a lad who had had only one year with Queen of the South.

The player I liked playing best with, and we had some other good ones such as Jacky Hather, Paddy Buckley and Tom Pearson, was young Harry Yorston. We seemed to have an immediate understanding, I always knew where he was and he knew where I could be found. It's a great plus in a colleague if he is always available for the ball.

We didn't have Joe O'Neil for the final and this was crucial. We had to play Jim Clunie, a centre half, at inside-left and although he tried very hard, he wasn't at ease in his new role. I don't think you can move players forward easily in football, it's much easier to take a step back. There may have been an element of thinking, "Well, we've thrashed Rangers, that's the Cup sewn up."

This was wrong. Celtic weren't one of the top Scottish clubs at that period but they had won the League that season and their half-back line was very powerful. Bobby Evans never stopped running and at centre-half they had a man called Jock Stein. He was comparatively unknown then but a good player and a very strong tackler. He played a very physical but very fair game. Perhaps the best of them was my immediate opponent that day, Bertie Peacock from Ireland. He too was a strong tackler but he could also use the ball.

Their cleverest player was Willie Fernie although you sometimes felt that he needed a ball to himself. However, it was his ability to hold the ball that brought Celtic their winner that day and we came back once more empty-handed. I had been given good news just before the final in that I had been picked against Norway and then to my amazement I was chosen to go to the World Cup in 1954. I have no idea why I was chosen and no idea why they didn't play me once we got to Switzerland. I remember sitting in the stand and feeling very sorry for big Fred Martin as Uruguay tore our defence to shreds and put seven in the net.

I greatly enjoyed my time with Aberdeen and felt they were a fine club to play with. Dave Halliday gave me lots of help when I was a young player as indeed had Willie Ferguson at Dumfries. I'm sure there was more humour in the game then, even when you were being hurt. Just after the war we had a great move in the Aberdeen side whereby Andy Cowie took a long throw, Archie Baird at the near post headed on and I came in to head home at the far post. We scored quite a few goals that way until I began to fail to get off the ground because a defender had a fistful of my jersey. Big Don Emery too was a caution, I never knew a harder kicker of the ball. I was once limping around at training, I had been injured and was in goals I think. Don came charging in on goal and thumped the ball against my shins and when I looked down they were already severely bruised.

I played a handful of games in our Championship season 1954-55 but not enough to quality for a medal. I was sorry to miss out on that. But I had the good fortune to play at international level with wonderful footballers like Billy Steel of Dundee and Jimmy Mason of Third Lanark. I enjoyed it all thoroughly and I would be very happy to be 22 or so and starting out all over again. I don't know how I'd do now, since we seem to have done away with wingers and I have to say that I think we have lost something in doing that.

CHAPTER FIVE

1959 v. ST MIRREN

THE AMERICAN, THE HEADMASTER AND THE FREE TRANSFER MAN

The year of 1959 was to provide one of the best summers ever recorded, two crops of strawberries and matches played on sun-baked pitches as late as October. It provided something else, the third totally non-Old Firm Cup Final in the space of three years and there indeed was a rarity.

The season 1958-59 had been an extremely worrying one for Aberdeen. For most of it, indeed for all of it, relegation had stared them squarely in the face. There could not be a more forbidding stare than having to win at Ibrox on the very last day of the season to remain in the First Division. Aberdeen managed to achieve this thanks to two goals from Norrie Davidson and in so doing appeared to have scuppered the championship aspirations of Rangers who needed to win to be sure of the title. They did win it but with muted rejoicings because they were indebted to their arch-rivals Celtic who at Parkhead that afternoon came from behind to deprive an all too nervous Hearts of a second championship in consecutive years.

For most of the five years since Aberdeen had last appeared in a Scottish Cup final, they had been managed by David Shaw, their former player who had taken over just after the Dons had taken the League Championship in 1955. This was a marvellous break-through for the club although the match which clinched the championship lacked the drama of the big Hampden occasion, being a comparatively low-key affair against Clyde at Shawfield. Subdued or not, Aberdeen had now joined the élite and could rank themselves with the big boys.

There were still a few familiar faces about. Fred Martin was back in goal although for the great bulk of the season he had not been the first choice and had played only some eight league games. Reggie Morrison had been the man preferred but lost his place in March and even more mysteriously left the staff by way of a free transfer in the close season. Davie Caldwell from Duntocher Hibs also survived from 1954 although he had moved over to right back and he was partnered by Jimmy Hogg from the Lothian Junior side, Preston Athletic. From the same part of the world came the right-half Ken Brownlee and Jim Clunie was bound to be more at home this time since his second final appearance would be in the role of centre-half, his proper and accustomed position. Archie Glen was at the peak of his powers and could be relied upon to spur the side from left-half.

The forward line was looking good. Dick Ewen was a local lad who had stepped up from Banks O' Dee to claim the right wing spot and his partner Norrie Davidson had done more than any other player to take the Dons to Hampden. He too had been an Aberdeenshire Junior with Inverurie Loco. The centre-forward had a chance of winning a medal very quickly because Hughie Baird had only arrived from Leeds United in the October and had cost £10,000, still a notable sum by the standards of the time. Bobby Wishart wore the number 10 jersey, a Dundee championship medal ahead of him, and Jacky Hather in his tenth year at Pittodrie would, like Fred Martin, make a third assault on a Scottish Cup medal.

Aberdeen had proceeded fairly sedately towards the final, being detained at Pittodrie by East Fife for longer than they would have wished to be in a 2-1 victory, but seeing off Arbroath comfortably at home, St Johnstone away and then Kilmarnock at home. Norrie Davidson scored in all these matches, three of them at home before gratifying crowds of 15,000, a profitable and comparatively stress-free Cup run.

The luck seemed to be still with the Dons with the announcement of the semi-final stage, for they had been drawn

against what most people would have regarded as the softest
option, Third Lanark. It didn't turn out that way. Thirds got a
battling 1-1 draw on the Saturday at Ibrox before 40,000 people.
Not too many Aberdonians made the return trip on the Wednesday to the same venue - there were only 18,000 there - but those
who did saw Davidson score as he had done four days before and
this time the goal was enough to book a final place. More to the
point, on the Saturday in the other semi-final, St Mirren had
bundled Celtic out with an ignominious score-line of 4-0, and
that could only be good news. It was not that Celtic in 1959
were a particularly strong side — they were not — but they
would undoubtedly have brought more history and presence to
a Scottish Cup Final than in the nature of things St Mirren were
able to do.

The Paisley side had to be regarded as one of the more
unusual to have reached the Scottish Cup Final in recent years,
not so much on the grounds of ability as in the strange circumstances in which they had been assembled. Indeed, the team
which started their league season in August 1958 did not bear
too much resemblance to the eleven which bore the black and
white stripes on that day in the following April.

In goal, Walker had taken over from Campbell Forsyth
as recently as March. Unlike Celtic, St Mirren were in the
business of making full backs out of centre-forwards. Davie
Lapsley, the Paisley skipper, and John Wilson, known to his
intimates as "Cockles", had both arrived at Love Street as
centre-forwards. The St Mirren right-half, Jackie Neilson, who
shared a Newtongrange Star background with his opposite
number Ken Brownlee, was one of the most experienced Paisley
players, having been there for ten years. He might need all his
experience to protect his young pivot, Jackie McGugan, who
had come only that season from Pollok. He was flanked on the
other side by Tommy Leishman, more mature than his five
years in the senior game would indicate.

It was the St Mirren forward line which had caused the
critics to take notice. Jim Rodger had never quite broken
through at Ibrox while a Rangers player, but he was big, strong
and fast. He had a particular superstition which consisted of
getting his hair cut in Glasgow University Union before every
Cup tie. This helpful hint had been passed on to him by Wilson
Humphries of Motherwell for whom it had worked very well in

1952 against Dundee. Tommy Bryceland at his left elbow was almost the only player of distinction ever produced by Gourock Juniors but he was distinguished indeed, needle-sharp and coolness itself in finishing.

Another recent signing had been the centre-forward Gerry Baker from Motherwell. He was one of two brothers who were both excellent strikers but both debarred from playing for Scotland because of the rigid qualification rules which then pertained. Both Gerry and his more famous brother Joe (of Hibernian, Arsenal and Nottingham Forest) had been brought up and educated in Scotland but Joe had been born in England, for which country he was later to play, and Gerry in the U.S.A. The Saints inside-left was Tommy Gemmell, a delightful inside-forward who used skill to thwart intimidation and who was possessed of almost saintly patience — perhaps appropriately, given his club — in the face of weekly fouling and harassment. The side was completed by the unsung Alistair Miller, a player that Third Lanark, after an unremarkable season, had decided that they could afford to let go on a free transfer.

The clubs had adopted different policies in the matter of pre-match arrangements. The Aberdeen caravanserai came to rest at Dunblane but Saints manager, Willie Reid, had decided that on balance the players would find it less upsetting if they spent the night preceding the match at home as usual and simply foregathered on the Saturday morning. On a dull, overcast Saturday morning with a hint of rain in the air, St Mirren struck the first blow for those who set store by such things — and most footballers did — when they managed to book the "lucky" home dressing room at Hampden.

Attracted by the prospect that there was unlikely to be any of the tedious and menacing nonsense associated with those finals of which the Old Firm formed part, an enormous crowd made its way out to Mount Florida. There were more than 108,000 people in the ground when Jack Mowat called the following teams to order:

ABERDEEN: Martin; Caldwell, Hogg, Brownlee, Clunie, Glen, Ewen, Davidson, Baird, Wishart, Hather.

ST. MIRREN: Walker; Lapsley, Wilson, Neilson, McGugan, Leishman, Rodger, Bryceland, Baker, Gemmell, Miller.

Astonishingly, twenty years after the outbreak of war in 1939, military service still had a part to play in this final. Two Aberdeen players, Jim Clunie and reserve Ian Burns, were on National Service in the R.A.F. and the Army respectively and required their Commanding Officers' permission to take part in the great occasion. Normally, the presentation of a couple of tickets to said Commanding Officers was an astute idea!

Davie Shaw took his seat, still simmering at a practical joke which had badly mis-fired in mid-week. He had received a telephone call which informed him that Norrie Davidson, who had scored in every round, had broken his leg and was nursing the injury at home. Shaw dashed round to the Davidson home to find out that Norrie indeed had a leg in plaster but that there was nothing wrong with it. Aberdeen University students, with more *joie de vivre* than sense, had done the deed as a stunt for the Charities Week. David Shaw, who rightly felt that in a Cup Final week managers had enough to contend with without this nonsense, was unable to extend any very charitable feelings towards "thae students". Still, that was in the past and Norrie Davidson had a chance to make it a goal in every round. So too for that matter had the opposition's Gerry Baker.

The outcome of the 1959 Cup Final absolutely turned on an early injury sustained by Dave Caldwell. He retired for attention, came back and crippled around for a few unavailing minutes before leaving the field for good. Aberdeen were forced to contemplate facing at least two-thirds of the game with a man short. It is true that the loss of a player can sometimes galvanise his remaining colleagues to extraordinary efforts, although it bears repeating that managers retain a firm preference for starting matches with the traditional eleven men.

Aberdeen however proceeded to aggravate this numerical loss by an ill-advised tactical switch. They decided to take the fast and tricky Hather out of the forward line and move him to right-back to replace directly the departed Caldwell. This was an error on two counts. Hather did not adjust quickly or particularly well to the new post of responsibility which had been thrust upon him and worse, from the Aberdeen point of view, it had been very apparent that while he was in his own position he had the pace and ability to worry Dave Lapsley who was a grizzled veteran and had in fact announced in the papers that the Cup Final would be his last game. To move Hather to defence was the equivalent of putting a Derby winner between the shafts of the local milk float.

Not surprisingly, the first half favoured St Mirren. Early on, Leishman had Martin scrambling with a shot which hit the bar and the big keeper did extremely well to stop a rasping shot from Rodger. Then disaster struck just when it looked as if Aberdeen might get to the interval unscathed. The same Rodger crossed from the right and Tommy Bryceland, with impeccable timing, glanced a header past Fred Martin which left the goalkeeper without a prayer.

A bad time to lose a goal, said the supporters, as if there were ever a good time, except perhaps three minutes to go and already 5-0 up. Yet it was easy to see what they meant. The ten minute interval, arrived at on terms of equality, would have provided a chance to take stock of the situation calmly and perhaps to redeploy forces, in a word to act rather than merely react to the situation.

Things got a bit tousier though never outrageously so in the second half as the rain began to spit. Jack Mowat, never one to reach precipitately for his wee black book, nevertheless found it necessary to take the names of Baker and Davidson, together with that of Hogg, all in separate incidents. The pace of Gerry Baker, which had so troubled the ageing Bobby Evans of Celtic in the semi-final, was beginning likewise to perturb the depleted Pittodrie defence and it was in the event to prove decisive.

He darted through the middle at great pace and got in his shot although heavily outnumbered by Martin, Glen and Clunie. Ironically, the defence was there in too great numbers, the three defenders collided and sprawled on the turf as Martin managed to block the shot. Even then, the ball could have gone anywhere but it bobbed gently across the open goal to the feet of Alistair Miller who, in the old Glasgow phrase, had time to comb his hair before scoring.

There was no way back from this second score and anything else would be by way of personal satisfaction or inadequate consolation. There was one goal in each category. Jim Clunie slipped on the increasingly greasy surface as he tried to control a through ball, allowing Baker to start for goal a yard up and that was all the American-born centre needed to pre-

1959 ABERDEEN v. ST MIRREN. Two goals down, frustration creeps into the play of the Dons. Here Norrie Davidson is about to be booked by referee Jack Mowat.

serve his record of having scored in every single round of the competition.

With a minute to go, when all spectator thoughts were turned to the presentation, Hugh Baird got a meaningless goal back for Aberdeen, the St Mirren defence's thoughts having likewise turned to the presentation. It is hard to score in a Cup final and find that your own supporters do not have the heart to applaud, nor indeed your colleagues the will to offer more than token congratulations.

St Mirren had deserved to win, even allowing for the injury to Dave Caldwell. Their approach had been more positive, their self-belief more marked. Dave Lapsley changed his mind about retiring. Jim Rodger became probably the only teacher in Scotland who in years to come, walking as Headmaster through the playground of his school, could trap a stray ball with the aplomb of one who had a Scottish Cup medal. The Paisley manager, Willie Reid, would end up for his efforts as manager of Norwich City after a terse interview in which he answered all the questions from the English Board with "I stand on my record".

A gratifying statistic was that there had not been a single arrest although there were more than 108,000 people in the ground. The supporters departed in different directions and in different moods. The black and white scarved contingent made the short journey to Cottonopolis, as the nineteenth century sports writers loved to call Paisley, and prepared for the victory procession and an incessant evening of *The Saints Go Marching In*. For the neutral, this was a hazard of such occasions. Two years later the return of the victorious Dunfermline Athletic to East End Park was accompanied from the beginning of the town boundary by a non-stop rendition of *The Happy Wanderer*.

The defeat marked the beginning of major changes at Pittodrie. A few months later, Davie Shaw demitted office. He had been player, trainer and manager and it is a measure of his unselfish commitment to the club that he now happily wielded sponge and towels again. His successor was the Pittodrie folk hero, Tommy Pearson, who for years baffled opponents with the Pearson double-shuffle, an even more refined version of the trickery with which in recent years Mark Walters has delighted crowds all over Scotland.

Dons would need a new goalkeeper, Fred Martin's 12 years or so were coming to a close. It was a great shame that so fine a club servant would not have a winner's medal to take into retirement with him. Sad too that the same could be said for that most popular of Englishmen, Jacky Hather, whose courage, speed and directness had well merited such an award.

Perhaps it all came back to that fateful positional change imposed by the injury to Caldwell. One of the truest sayings in football is that hindsight has twenty-twenty vision but the redeployment of Hather did seem to have tipped the scales. The astringent Cyril Horne certainly was of that belief: "I am sure that Aberdeen could have tackled the problem much more intelligently; it certainly was rank bad strategy to permit a full-back so lacking in mobility as Lapsley an hour of welcome leisure."

Perhaps. What was certain is that it was high time that Aberdeen acquired the winning habit at Hampden again, they had lost the last three in a row and there would be further disappointment before the tide turned. By the time the Northern legions came back to the classic slopes, becoming steadily less classical with the years, they would be singing Beatles songs and the mini skirt would be about to win general acceptance. In 1959 Eddie Calvert, the Man with the Golden Trumpet, was available as top of the bill at the Empire to console Aberdonians with a musical turn of mind. The Empire itself would be gone by 1967 and so too would the vast majority of the dozen cinemas which on that day in 1959 could still be found within a mile's walk of Hampden Park. It was perhaps cruelly symbolic that on that damp evening, as the squads moved in to remove the tons of litter from the soaked Hampden terracings, two of those cinemas were showing *Room at the Top*.

The old saying that victory has many fathers but failure is an orphan was starkly emphasised by the circumstances of Aberdeen's return to their own city. They came by train, the last time they would do so, and their disembarkation was described thus: "Not a sound was heard, not a cheer raised or a glad shout at the sight of a familiar face. Silently the handful of spectators saw the Dons dribble in ones and twos from the compartment, mingle with the other train travellers and quietly leave the station." Perhaps the result at Ibrox the previous week had been the more important one and Bobby Calder was out scouting.

1959 — FRED MARTIN REMEMBERS

The thing I remember about the 1953 final was the injury to George Niven. Big George Young went into goal but he wasn't a complete novice there. I remember he had gone into goal once in a match at Pittodrie when George Niven was also injured. Personally I wasn't too over-awed by the occasion, we had played Celtic at Hampden a couple of years before in the Festival of Britain Cup final and there was a very big crowd there for that.

We probably lost the game on the first match although Harry Yorston gave us the chance to replay with his late equaliser. People thought in those days that you only got one chance at Celtic or Rangers and I think that was probably right. It was time-consuming and expensive to come down from Aberdeen in those days and our support was a few thousand down on the Wednesday night, very important if you consider that a Hampden final is all intents and purposes a home match for the Old Firm. In a sense we were a bit lucky to get to the final because we had been terrible in the semi-final against Third Lanark. I always found semi-finals very tense because you are so nearly there and even if you lose the final itself you have had all the enjoyment of the big day.

The next year, 1954, we approached with great confidence because we had beaten Rangers 6-0 in the semi-final. I don't think we were over-confident, but we knew we had a very good side and that was proved by the fact that we won the championship the following season. People say that we lost the final because of the absence through injury of Joe O'Neil but although he had a marvellous match against Rangers Joe was at the time really a fringe player. Celtic's first goal was unfortunate as I had Mochan's shot covered but Alex Young who was nearer the ball tried to play it, as he had to do. He did not get a clean contact and the ball swerved away from me to the other side of the net. It shows that football is a strange game when the winner was scored by Sean Fallon, who was very strong and willing but whose ball control didn't match that of any of our forwards. But that's football. My memory of Jock Stein is not so much from this match as from an earlier League game at Pittodrie. Jock was pretty slow and all down the left side and Paddy Buckley was giving him such a hard time that suddenly we noticed that Buckley's shorts had come adrift, ripped from top to bottom where Jock had a grip of them!

My last final was that of 1959. We felt we must have a good chance because for once we were playing not a member of the Old Firm, but St Mirren, and they were a side we almost always did well against in the League matches. However, the week before we had had a very draining game against Rangers at Ibrox when we had to win to stay up in the First Division and although we did win I feel the game took a lot out of us. I remember walking off the pitch at Ibrox with Jimmy Hogg and we were hugging each other, the crowd was booing fiercely because they thought Rangers had thrown away the championship. We weren't bothered, because we had won, they could boo all they liked. Suddenly there was a tremendous surge of cheering as the crowd learned that Hearts, who had been winning 1-0 at Parkhead, had gone down 2-1. Celtic had won the League for Rangers!

In the 1959 final itself, everything turned on the injury to Caldwell. I couldn't believe it when the manager, Davie Shaw, decided on moving Jackie Hather from left wing to right back. It was a terrible switch for several reasons. First of all Hather had been scudding past their right back Davie Lapsley who was short of pace. Secondly, Jackie was fast and direct as a forward, with a wonderful shot but in defence he was a non-tackler and quite unable to head the ball. He was quite liable to give away a penalty if he challenged in the box because he did not know how to tackle properly. It would have been a much better decision to move Bobby Wishart to the right back spot, he had played there before in emergencies and he had done well there.

We lost the first goal on the stroke of half-time. It had just begun to drizzle and little Tommy Bryceland got up to head a cross from Archie Gemmell. There was no great pace on it, it was a floater but as I pushed off for it my right foot went and I couldn't get to the ball. I remember that at half-time in the dressing room Teddy Scott said to me "I hope those studs of yours are O.K." I can't remember the second goal but for the third Gerry Baker was clean through. He had the ball and I didn't and he just clipped it over me to the net.

We didn't think much about the rights and wrongs of substitutes, in those days it was just the way the game was played. Occasionally, if I got an arm knock in goal, I would finish the game as an outside player for I was reasonably skilful having started as an inside-forward when I signed from Carnoustie Panmure. The timing of St Mirren's first goal was crucial that day. They had a good forward line but we were containing them well even with ten men and their forwards were beginning to feel a bit frustrated, we could see Gerry Baker and Tommy Bryceland niggling at each other. They liked to play short one-twos, good players both, while Tommy Gemmell was a very stylish player. He played deeper and used the long ball more.

There were a lot of good players about then. Ed Turnbull was always under-rated, he was the power-house of the Hibernian attack. Gordon Smith was a great player too although of course he was fully acknowledged as such. The three Hearts players, Conn, Bauld and Wardhaugh, were outstanding and yet I don't suppose they had a dozen caps between them. We always felt that if you were picked for Scotland and weren't an Old Firm player then you must be really good! Graham Leggatt for instance would certainly have been picked earlier and more often for Scotland had he played for one of the big Glasgow clubs.

Yet for all the good players here I realised when I played against the Uruguayans in the summer of 1954 and the Hungarians in the same year that I had never really played football up until then. Players like Schiaffino of Uruguay and Puskas and Hidgekuti of Hungary were truly from another dimension altogether. The World Cup of 1954 was farcical, I know that all things evolve with time but we had only 13 players and one goalkeeper, me.

We had had an unfortunate run-up to Switzerland because in a warm-up match against Norway, I think there were three Aberdeen players picked, the first time that had happened, Paddy Buckley got a cartilage injury and he was never the same player after that. He was lightning quick, Jock Stein would testify to that.

I had the strong feeling that the 1959 Cup Final would possibly be my last chance, I'd already been 13 years at Pittodrie by that time. The following September, playing in a match against Dundee at Pittodrie, I had my jaw broken. I was out until Christmas, came back and played one or two matches but from then on I was in the Reserves almost all the time and the following season I decided to call it a day. But there is no doubt that for those four years or so in the mid 1950s Aberdeen were a very good side indeed. We won the League and the League Cup and we probably SHOULD have won the Scottish Cup at least once.

CHAPTER SIX

1967 v. CELTIC

EATEN BY THE LIONS

T here is a curious symmetry about the meetings of Aberdeen and Celtic in Scottish Cup finals. They had encountered each other there in both Coronation years and would be in opposition in each of the two seasons in which Celtic found themselves at the last stage of the greatest club competition of all, the European Cup.

To be drawn against Celtic in that year of 1967 was rather like standing in the middle of a railway track and hoping that you had been endowed with the powers of Superman to stop the approaching express train. The Parkhead juggernaut, to mix transport metaphors, had rolled on remorselessly since the autumn, detained neither by foreign or home-grown opposition. The Celtic manager, Jock Stein, had now been at Parkhead for two years and had worked out exactly what each of his squad was capable of doing.

The season's league matches had been reasonably productive for the Dons and they had finished a good if not particularly close fourth in the table. Their rate of striking, 72 goals in 34 matches, was likewise satisfactory although in winning the championship, Celtic would score no fewer than 111 goals and thus achieve the very rare feat of averaging more than three goals per game.

In the Cup itself, Aberdeen seemed unable to escape the Tayside connection. To be drawn against Dundee in the first round was potentially dangerous and Pittodrie fans were glad of the home advantage conferred by the tie. As occasionally happens, a potentially hazardous match presented no difficulty at all and Aberdeen skated home by five clear goals. That was the margin in the next round when they went up river to Perth and calmly disposed of St Johnstone. A struggling draw against Hibernian at Easter Road in the quarter-final was redeemed by their best performance of the season to date when they won the replay comfortably in Aberdeen. The slight break of fortune which every cup side needs came their way when in the semi-final against Dundee United, the latter's Tommy Millar was sufficiently unlucky to score an own goal when it seemed unlikely that either side would ever manage this in the ortho-dox manner, Aberdeen even having spurned a penalty kick.

It was eight years since Aberdeen had last been at Hampden for the Scottish Cup Final and, expectedly, none of the 1959 players had survived the long gap. Bobby Clark would be in goal and on familiar ground. He had started with Queen's Park when Eddie Turnbull was coach at Hampden — Queen's Park did not have managers in the strict sense — and when Turnbull took on the Aberdeen manager's job in 1965, he took Clark north with him. He would play behind a pair of gritty, serviceable full backs, Jimmy Whyte and Ally Shewan.

The mid-field was in the charge of Frank Munro, taken from Dundee United, Tommy McMillan and the languidly elegant Jens Petersen, one of the many Scandinavian players who contributed so much grace and artistry to the more home-spun Scottish game in the 1960s. Hal Stewart of Morton had led the way with Jerry Kerr of Dundee United in tapping this rich vein of skill, and now Aberdeen were prospecting on their own account.

Up front the Dons, it was thought, could more than look after themselves. Two of the five, Jim Storrie and Harry Melrose, already knew all about the Cup finals. Storrie had been in the Leeds United side that took Liverpool to extra time in the F.A. Cup Final of 1965 and even then it had needed a goal from another Scot — Ian St John — to beat him. Harry Melrose had been in Jock Stein's Dunfermline side which created one of the greatest shocks in Cup Final history when it defeated

Celtic in a replay in 1961. Four years later Harry, still with the Fife side, had seen a second medal snatched away from him by a late Celtic recovery under the direction of that very same Jock Stein. For both men, therefore, this third Final meeting would be in the nature of a rubber match.

Every so often, Aberdeen delved deep into the West of Scotland and came up with an extraordinarily talented inside-forward. They had done it with Willie Mills, they had done it with Charlie Cooke and now in Jimmy Smith, they had just such another. Fairly tall for that position with a hint of the pale and under-nourished about him, he had the fierce desire for possession which marks the born ball player. On the flanks little Jimmy Wilson would prove that he was versatile as well as fast and elusive by taking the right-wing spot, whereas in the semi-final he had occupied the left. The new wearer of the number 11 jersey, Dave Johnston, was never going to be faulted for lack of effort.

The Aberdeen manager, Eddie Turnbull, was one of the most fiercely competitive people in Scottish or for that matter British football. He was not the kind of man to be over-awed or intimidated by a scrutiny of the ranks of the enemy. Just as well, for the forces arranged against him could reasonably have daunted the stoutest of hearts.

Celtic had as goalkeeper Ronnie Simpson who had, like Bobby Clark, begun his senior career at Hampden but in his case an astonishing 22 years before, when he had made his debut against Clyde as a fourteen year old. Arriving at Parkhead almost by accident after a distinguished career with Newcastle United and Hibernian, he proved the final link that the Celtic defence had required. In a curious contradiction he kept goal in a most composed way while always appearing wracked by anxiety.

The backs were Jim Craig and Tommy Gemmell, Craig the speedy overlapper in the modern mould, capable of delivering the precise cross and not infrequently the accurate shot, Gemmell the ebullient extrovert who let no occasion, however important, get to him. He was one man who would not be afflicted by nerves on the day. The defence was built around Billy McNeill who laid claim to everything in the air and would eventually as manager take an Aberdeen side to a Cup final. On either side of him were Bobby Murdoch, unexcelled in the

1967 ABERDEEN v. CELTIC. Simpson clears off the line with an effective if inelegant fly hack.

dissecting pass, and John Clark, the player that Jock Stein himself regarded as the crucial element in the rear guard.

Most of the forwards had been there when Stein arrived, it had been a matter of re-arranging them. On the right wing was a truly extraordinary talent, the small, brave, lightning-quick Jimmy Johnstone. Men as small as he were expected to be elusive and tricky. What was unlooked-for was that he would be able to outjump much taller defenders or that he would have a power of shot breath-taking in such a diminutive player. Willie Wallace was as lethal in the penalty area as the man he had been called in to replace, Joe McBride. The saturnine Bertie Auld was the Mephistopheles of the front file, always thinking and the provider of well-judged passes for Lennox and Chalmers. Bobby Lennox had an unrivalled acceleration from a standing start and no player ever suffered more from erroneous offside decisions. Steve Chalmers provided one of the strangest cases of late football development. In his late twenties he made the transition from good average First Division player to European-class club man and internationalist on merit.

Still, even the best side can play only as well as the opposition will let it, and Aberdeen were entitled to approach the final with hopes high. For one thing, Celtic had had a hectic few days in the run-up to the Hampden match and that might tell against them. They had been in Prague, defending a first-leg lead against Dukla in the European Cup semi-final and for the first and perhaps only time, Celtic had played a naked, defensive game. Naked but not unashamed because Robert Kelly had denounced such tactics and even Jock Stein himself was most apologetic about it when discussing the match in later years. It had worked, a 0-0 draw would take Celtic to Lisbon and the team had given sufficient proof of its commitment to all-out attacking football to be allowed one lapse. One thing was sure, Celtic would be more aggressive come the Scottish Cup Final.

There had been a good Aberdeen performance in a recent League match at Parkhead to draw comfort from when the Dons had rather the better of a goal-less draw and might have improved on that had Jimmy Wilson been able to put away a couple of chances that fell to him. The concentration on the Old Firm — Rangers were likewise making their way to the

1967 ABERDEEN v. CELTIC. Steve Chalmers has to double back in defence to help out his hard-pressed goalkeeper, Ronnie Simpson.

final of the Cup Winners' Cup — kept the domestic final largely off the sports pages but for Aberdeen this might be no bad thing. Glasgow sides have always got the lion's share of attention in any such run-up so the Pittodrie officials were not displeased with the comparative shortage of column inches as players and officials gathered at Gleneagles.

In public, Eddie Turnbull sounded genuinely optimistic in his pronouncements to newspapers, radio and television:

"We will give them as hard a match as they've had this season and we will play to win without the need of a replay. We have the players, the skill, and the will to win. We will have the champagne at the ready."

Brave words, but the bookmakers, going solely on things past and form shown, had decided that Aberdeen were identifiably underdogs at 4-1. They would not lack for support from the large crowd of 126,000 and in addition to the normal conveyance by train, bus, plane and car, there was a whiff of possible criminality. A Singer Gazelle went missing in Aberdeen itself and the police in the West of Scotland were asked to keep a wary eye for it, in case the thieves might fancy a jaunt to Hampden.

The presentations were made, the National Anthem played, the military bands wound their interminable way from the field and up the sloping track by the eastern end of the grandstand. The referee got the game under way to the accompaniment of that great surging roar from the terracing that always accompanied the first sideways tap of the ball.

ABERDEEN: Clark; Whyte, Shewan, Munro, McMillan, Petersen, Wilson, Smith, Storrie, Melrose, Johnston.

CELTIC: Simpson; Craig, Gemmell, Murdoch, McNeill, Clark, Johnstone, Wallace, Chalmers, Auld, Lennox.

The Dons were entitled to hope that the trip to Prague in midweek would have left some Celtic players at least physically or mentally fatigued. It had been a long journey and they had been required to play a tactical game which they neither liked nor were particularly well-equipped to play. There was likewise the hope that the Parkhead side would have an off-day. They were not supermen after all, just eleven very good players. Second Division side Queen's Park had given them all sorts of trouble in the quarter-final, scoring three goals on Celtic's own ground and it was only with a handful of minutes to go that Celtic got the fifth goal which finally tilted the match away from the gallant Hampden side.

But 1967 was to be Celtic's year and, in the eternal if fruitless search for ifs and buts, it might just not have been, had this been a battle of the managers. Jock Stein was in his appointed place but Eddie Turnbull was missing. Overnight, he had taken ill at Gleneagles and was in considerable distress. He was desperate to attend and made every effort to do so — indeed Aberdeen waited so long on him that they ended up by executing an undignified dash to Hampden, arriving out of breath and flustered much later than they would ideally have wished to do. Turnbull did not make it and Aberdeen were deprived of his observant eye.

A side of the abundant and rampaging forward talent of Celtic — they had left out John Hughes who scored five goals in a League match against Aberdeen — were always liable to run riot and score a hatful of goals. It was probably fear of this which led Aberdeen to commit the cardinal error of worrying about what the opposition were doing, rather than attempting to dictate the flow of the match themselves.

One man on the Aberdeen side was perhaps rather more relaxed than his fellow team-mates, goalkeeper Bobby Clark. He was at that time a student at the Scottish School of Physical Education located at Jordanhill College in Glasgow and he had spent the previous day with his fellow students engaged in learning the art of canoeing on Loch Lomond, a risky venture which could not have improved the manager's state of health.

The Dons almost wilfully discarded their trump card. Harry Melrose was pulled back into mid-field to stop Murdoch and Auld running the show. So too, much more damagingly, was Jimmy Smith and the gangling inside-forward was lost in the obscure territorial battles which were being waged there. One of his tackles on Steve Chalmers was construed by the referee as being too literally battling and with the fear of another such and a sending-off looming, Smith made no further impact on the game. There were strong parallels with the failure of Willie Mills to dominate in 1937. In the course of the whole ninety minutes, Aberdeen threatened on but two occasions. On the first of them a half-hit Storrie shot was rolling in but Tommy Gemmell got back and scraped it off the line, grinning hugely, and in the other instance a Petersen shot looked like escaping Simpson but he recovered to kick it clear, a feature of the Celtic goalkeeper's technique being his willingness to use any part of his anatomy that presented itself.

It was a clean, quick kill for the goals that finished Aberdeen off arrived with arithmetical precision three minutes either side of half-time. They had been well and truly sign-posted by near-incessant Celtic attacks. Almost on the stroke of half-time, probing work by Johnstone, who had been encouraged by Stein to desert his wing and raid through the centre, forced Aberdeen to concede a corner. Auld worked a short corner with Lennox, gave the latter the ball back and Lennox gave the lie to those who thought him simply a dasher by laying the ball neatly in front of Wallace and inviting him to pick out a square of netting. Wallace duly identified same and drove the ball home without fuss. It was a devastating goal scored at a devastating time and it seemed unlikely that Turnbull, had he been there, would not have said something very forceful and to the point at half-time.

On this day, however, Aberdeen were rudderless and interest in the match did not survive their return to the field by more than three minutes. Again, a Celtic player cutting in from the wing, this time Johnstone, again the precision cut-back and this time, for variety, Wallace drove it high into the net. The game was finished and everybody knew it. In an irreverent parody of the dismissal blessing in the Catholic Church, a massive Celtic supporter stood up and bellowed to all and sundry: "You may go, the match is ended". Ended it was, although having 42 minutes yet to run. Celtic continued to attack but without seeming over-committed to adding to their goal tally which in a perverse way was more humiliating for the Dons than an out and out drubbing would have been.

High in the Press Box above Hampden, two men were filing their reports, each sure that he knew why the game had gone the way it did, each reaching remarkably similar conclusions. Gair Henderson of the *Evening Times* explained why Celtic had won the Scottish Cup and Aberdeen were still seeking their second victory:

"Aberdeen were set in their ways. They play to a pattern. If things come off well and good, but if they don't they are like the leopard, totally unable to change its spots." On the

1967 CELTIC v. ABERDEEN. FIRST BLOOD TO CELTIC. The combined attentions of three Dons, Shewan, Clark and Whyte, are not enough to prevent Willie Wallace putting Celtic ahead from a slip by Bobby Lennox.

sister paper, the *Glasgow Herald*, Glyn Edwards expressed basically the same sentiments more eloquently:

"Aberdeen's unrealistic dedication to caution withdrew Smith and Melrose and led to a voluntary under-manning of their attack."

Under-manning and under-mining. The Dons would not win another Cup until they were prepared to chance everything, that was a lesson which Turnbull realised he must teach them. The Marquis of Montrose was not an Aberdeen supporter, indeed he put the town to the sword in 1644, but he wrote a poem which contained a recipe for the winning of the Scottish Cup:

"He either fears his fate too much
  Or his deserts are small
  Who puts it not unto the touch
  To win or lose it all."

Football can be a cruel game but it does provide its own anaesthetic. Aberdeen had to forget about a defeat all the more painful because they had not done themselves justice, and get down to Kilmarnock to play a League match on the Monday night. There they got a respectable 1-1 draw despite missing another penalty (Jim Storrie had missed one at Dundee in the semi-final) but were saved on this occasion because in trying to clear the rebound, Jackie McGrory of Kilmarnock obligingly knocked the ball into his own net.

And perhaps, with the benefit of the historical perspective, there was no beating Celtic that year anyhow. Their battle honours list was awesome, League, League Cup, Scottish Cup, Glasgow Cup, and three weeks later the European Cup in Lisbon, a success which sent the bristle-haired Bill Shankly running to Stein in the Celtic dressing-room with the famous cry "John, you're immortal!"

Of the two goalkeepers, Clark would have another chance at a medal and although Simpson would not, there was consolation in abundance in Portugal and the further bonus of making an international debut at the record age of 37, a win at Wembley moreover against the World Cup champions, England. As someone said to Ian Botham on a similar occasion, "Who writes your scripts?"

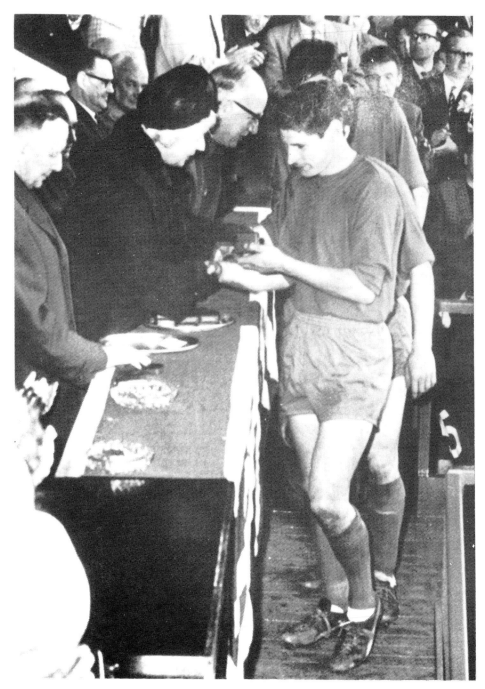

1967 ABERDEEN v. CELTIC. It's a weary trail up the Hampden steps for a loser's medal but Ally Shewan manages to put a brave face on it.

Two players had the nick-name "Jinky" that day, Johnstone and Smith, but the Celtic player was to know infinitely greater success. Jimmy Smith was to prove one of that numerous category, a great potential talent never quite realised. Frank Munro would later turn out for Celtic but with minimal success at a time of Parkhead upheaval.

So ended the third final between Aberdeen and Celtic. It seemed that at that stage the two sides could not be kept apart and so it proved, because three years later the Dons were to gain their second Scottish Cup success in one of the most explosive finals of all time.

1967 — JIMMY WILSON REMEMBERS

I have no doubt at all that Eddie Turnbull's illness cost us the Scottish Cup that year. It was not so much his not being there as the way in which we learned of it. He had taken training at Pittodrie on the Friday morning and seemed quite O.K. so that when we set off for Gleneagles in the afternoon the last thing on our minds was that he would not be at Hampden.

We were told he could not be going about 12.30 p.m. on the Saturday and we were all summoned to his room. It was a huge bedroom and I remember thinking it was like being called in to see a dying king. We gathered round the bed but I can't remember anything he may have said to us then.

To make matters worse, the bus we travelled down to Glasgow in actually got lost and we arrived at Hampden just over half an hour before the kick-off. Eddie would have taken care to ensure we didn't get there too early anyway but half an hour was a bit fine, especially when you think you are lost.

We weren't in any particular awe of Celtic. The previous year we had ended a run of 24 unbeaten matches for them when we won at Pittodrie and only ten days or so beforehand we had the better of a drawn match at Parkhead. But on the day we didn't play at all and this is where Turnbull's absence was vital. He had taught us to believe that we were as good as any side and was particularly good at winding us up for big occasions. Maybe too good, we had two orderings-off and 35 bookings in that season, a lot for those days.

If we had known about his absence sooner, then one of the senior players, maybe our captain Harry Melrose, could have taken charge effectively and worked out some alternative plan but Eddie was a great manager in that he had very clear ideas of what he wanted his team to do, and latterly he did not want anyone to argue with him about it. As it was, the only direction we got was when a couple of directors came into the dressing room at half time and even then they only said things like "Wingers, run fast!" We thought we were doing that anyway and it simply irritated us.

They (Celtic) were a very good side. So were we, but on the day we just didn't play and I don't think in any case we had anybody as good as Jimmy Johnstone or Bertie Auld. After all, they won everything they went for that year. Towards the end Bertie and Bobby Murdoch began to take the mickey with close passing but by that time all we wanted to do was to get the game over.

Years later I was with some of the Celtic boys and said to Jock Stein that we would have won if Eddie Turnbull had been there. John Clark got quite indignant and said "It's got nothing to do with the manager". I laughed and said to Stein "Do you hear that, Jock, nine in a row has got nothing to do with you?" John Clark then realised what he had said but Jock Stein just laughed.

We had a reception of some kind after the game, but I don't remember much about it, it was more like a wake. We were very down, not because we had been beaten, but because we knew that we had totally failed to play as we could do. All I wanted was to get out there again and show that I could do a lot better than that.

Because of the way it worked out I didn't actually enjoy the day very much. It was the second time I had played before a six-figure crowd at Hampden — for Morton against Rangers in a League Cup final was the other one — and I remember how both Celtic and Rangers could wait and then pounce.

I wasn't at Aberdeen for much longer. In December I played in both Cup Winners Cup matches against Standard Liège. We lost 3-0 in Belgium although we got it back to a 3-2 aggregate at Pittodrie. Eddie Turnbull then decided it was time to rebuild his team, he was always a great man for rebuilding. I went to Dundee and almost got a League Cup Final medal when they beat Celtic but I missed out on the final itself. I often think back on what might have happened if the manager hadn't become ill so suddenly.

CHAPTER SEVEN

1970 v. CELTIC

DREAMS AND OMENS

The two clubs which had contested the Scottish Cup Final of 1967 were back again at Hampden just three years later. Despite that, there were only two survivors in the Aberdeen side, goalkeeper Bobby Clark and centre-half Tommy McMillan. This pair, with nine others new to Hampden, would face the daunting assignment of bettering a Celtic side which had won almost everything in sight in the interim and now looked set to repeat its European triumph of 1967. What is rather more surprising is that there would be five changes in the Celtic side but then over the nine year period of almost unbroken success, Stein changed his team radically not once but twice, so that only Billy McNeill and Bobby Lennox would go every step of the championship road.

Eddie Turnbull was still manager and this time he would be at Hampden. He had already made up his mind that whatever else happened, Aberdeen's approach would be positive, and so it turned out in one of the most turbulent finals ever. If for no other reason, and freely conceding that on the day the refereeing decisions went Aberdeen's way, Aberdeen deserved their much-deferred second Scottish Cup success.

Their League performance had once again been indifferent and they were embedded in the middle of the table. Nor was their Cup run to date anything to write odes about, a comfortable 4-0 win against Clyde had been followed by single goal victories against Clydebank at home (a dire performance), Falkirk away and in the semi-final Kilmarnock at the now-vanished Muirton Park, Perth. This was an odd venue for a national semi-final, the fact that there were fewer than 3,000 stand seats available to spectators would in itself have made it so. Possibly as a result, the match never caught fire and the only memory the author has of it — he was doing the television commentary on the match — is of the speed with which Derek McKay put away the one clear-cut chance that fell to him, in fact the memory is not only of the speed but also of the certainty with which the ball was dispatched. Here was a lad for commentators to note and for opponents to mark.

It is time to look at the teams in detail. Bobby Clark, as has been mentioned, was still in goal, he would be at the centre of one of the most controversial moments of the afternoon. The huge Dane, Henning Boel, was at right back — or more accurately perhaps wearing the number 2 shirt since such tight allocations of positions were becoming more and more unfashionable. Next came George Murray, Jim Hermiston who after years of policing forwards returned to police the general public, and Tommy McMillan.

The captain was Martin Buchan, barely 21 years old but one of nature's leaders. He was scholarly in the way that cricket followers would recognise Mike Brearley or Peter Roebuck to be scholarly. The lad who reads a book in the team bus when he doesn't have to is not necessarily the most popular of mortals with his colleagues but Martin was heavily endowed with talent and his performances on-field were such that he could read whenever and whatever he wanted to.

In front of him he had the recently-introduced Derek McKay who had made no impression during his time with Dundee at Dens Park. He had been crucial in the Cup-winning run and his team-mates noted that his confidence increased in direct proportion to the importance of the game. He had told his fellow lodger, Joe Harper, that not only would Aberdeen win but that he himself would score. It was a nice, relaxed attitude to take into a Cup final.

Davie Robb was strong, difficult to dislodge as he hunched

over the ball and the owner of a strong shot and a cool head. He also abundantly LIKED playing football, a quality which by no means every professional footballer possesses, or if he possesses it, seems able to convey. The author's last glimpse of Robb was of his playing in the Houston Astrodrome in the North American Soccer League and of his being at least two classes above anyone else on the field, with the possible exception of the former England player, Frank Worthington. The remaining players were Jim Forrest, Joe Harper and Arthur Graham. Forrest had been a consistently heavy scorer with Rangers until, with George McLean, he was most unjustly handed personal responsibility for the Ibrox side's shock defeat at Berwick in the Scottish Cup of 1967. With his cousin, Alex Willoughby, he came north — by way of Preston in Forrest's case — and they would both have played in the Final, had not Willoughby sustained an injury. Joe Harper had been discovered for Morton by that knowledgeable football man, Hal Stewart. Short, almost tubby — invariably referred to by opposing supporters as a barrel of something or other, never complimentary — Harper was in love with scoring goals and there have been few greater favourites at Pittodrie. These two, Forrest and Harper, would give even one of the best defences in Europe — perhaps the very best — something to think about. Last of the Dons was the young Arthur Graham, another in the long line of Glaswegians snatched from the Big Two and at 17 years of age, the Castlemilk lad had to be one of the youngest finalists ever.

And the opposition, what of them? Ronnie Simpson had gone from goal, a shoulder injury had done for him eventually at the age of 38, despite a gallant effort at a come-back. Evan Williams now wore the keeper's jersey, a reliable last-line who in that curious way that football sometimes has, never quite seemed to win the unqualified affection of the Celtic support. David Hay, strong as a horse but much more subtle, was at right-back, he would be one of the two Celtic players in that side to retire prematurely from the playing side, in his case because of the lingering effects of an eye injury. He was also one of the two future Celtic managers in the side. Tommy Gemmell was still there, likewise Bobby Murdoch and Billy McNeill, but Jim Brogan would be the man to take the place of John Clark. Jimmy Johnstone, Willie Wallace and Bobby Lennox were carry-overs from 1967 but the other two were of more than passing interest.

George Connelly had been cast for greatness since the time when as a fourteen year old, he had given an astounding exhibition of ball-juggling during the interval of a European match at Celtic Park. He had every quality that a footballer could hope to have, a fine shot, the ability to read a game, mastery of the telling pass and instant control of the ball no matter the height, no matter the angle. What he could not cope with were the pressures of being a top-class footballer and gradually his absences from training became more frequent, his omissions from the first team inevitable. By the time he was in his mid-20s and when he should still have had another 10 years ahead of him, he had effectively removed himself from first-class football.

All that was in the future, however, and what he had done, in that spring of 1970, was to go a long way to remove Leeds United from the European Cup by scoring the only goal in the first leg of the semi-final at Elland Road.

John Hughes was a great imponderable. He was big, over six feet and built accordingly so that at first glance he might be slotted in as a centre-forward of the old-fashioned type. In fact he was possessed of considerable speed which he used to good effect raiding wide on the left. His release of the final pass was not always well judged, Bertie Auld's reactions were proof of that, but Hughes could trouble the most famous of centre-halves and indeed had distinctly the better of Jackie Charlton in his half-dozen or so encounters with the Leeds and England centre-half.

Eddie Turnbull knew that on the day Aberdeen had to play the opposing team rather than a reputation. A few days before, something had happened which had lifted spirits in the Pittodrie camp. Aberdeen had gone to Parkhead to play Celtic in a league match which would give the Glasgow side their fifth championship in a row, were they to win it. They lost 2-1 to an Aberdeen side in which Arthur Graham intimated by-ordinary promise and the flag did not arrive at Parkhead just yet. Wrong to make too much of an isolated result of course, but Aberdeen had won on Celtic's ground in a match in which the home side had most definitely been trying.

Aberdeen were a well-turned out lot off the field. Breakfasting at Gleneagles on the Saturday morning, a visiting American had been so impressed by the appearance of the players in club blazers and slacks that he assumed they were some kind of choir. Joe Harper, who must have been startled to have been taken for a choirboy, put him right whereon the American offered them a party that night on their way back from the game.

Jock Stein meanwhile was endeavouring to keep his players' minds off Europe for the time being. In his gruff, terse style, he declaimed:

"The Scottish Cup is not going to be sacrificed because we are due to play Leeds United next Wednesday."

Nor would he have been best pleased to see that his side were quoted at 5-2 on with Aberdeen at a generous 5-1 against. Such odds might well induce complacency among his players, and his players would know the odds.

The crowd was 108,000, the referee was R.H. Davidson, and these were the teams:

ABERDEEN: Clark; Boel, Murray, Hermiston, McMillan, M. Buchan, McKay, Robb, Forrest, Harper, Graham. Substitute: G. Buchan

CELTIC: Williams; Hay, Gemmell, Murdoch, McNeill, Brogan, Johnstone, Wallace, Connelly, Lennox, Hughes. Substitute: Auld

A few final points need to be made about team selection, the first being that since 1967 teams had been allowed to introduce a substitute, only one at first. Aberdeen's selection of George Buchan for this role meant that two brothers were potentially playing in a Scottish Cup final for the first time since Frank and Hugh O'Donnell had done so for Celtic in the early 1930s. It might have been thought too that any side as successful as the Celtic one of that time would more or less pick itself, but this was far from the case. In the run-up to the final, Celtic played 18 different teams in the last 18 games. Stein did this for two reasons, the more obvious of which was to keep the opposition guessing. There was an element too, however, of never allowing his own players to take a place for granted.

The Aberdeen victory of 1970 has been partially overshadowed by the furore which attached itself to the referee that day. That is unfortunate and in a real sense unfair because it has tended to obscure the standard of performance by the Dons that afternoon against one of the truly great European sides of the day. There were three crucial decisions and each of them went

SEVEN

ABERDEEN · FINAL EDITION

Aberdeen's way. The first came in 27 minutes when a cross from Derek McKay — it was going to be impossible to keep his name out of the match report — was driven against the arm of a Celtic defender. The latter's identity varied but Bobby Murdoch topped the poll of probables. It did not seem likely that Murdoch could have got his arm out of the way, and certainly there was no concerted appeal from the Aberdeen players.

There was the father and mother of a concerted protest from the Celtic players, and it was a genuine one, not the simulated indignation which so often accompanies such demonstrations. Mr Davidson was not for turning and the award stood, but so vehement were the protests that before it could be taken, Tommy Gemmell had to be booked.

Joe Harper was the Aberdeen player designated to take any penalties that might be given and in an interview fourteen years later, he recalled how he had felt it vital to get hold of the ball during the protracted rammy that followed the award. He describes how he juggled with it on the spot for seven minutes — a pardonable but Homeric exaggeration — and then struck the ball to where he had decided it would go, the right hand of goalkeeper Evan Williams who was left half-sitting in an extremely undignified position as the ball passed him.

Aberdeen one up then and a bit fortunate at that. Celtic, fuming, were put in an even worse temper when Bobby Lennox appeared to dispossess a nervous and hesitant Bobby Clark only to find the goal disallowed for a foul on the Aberdeen goalkeeper which few had seen. Bobby Clark was a splendid goalkeeper but did have two faults in technique. The more frequent one was that he was a notably bad kicker of a dead ball, something which not even Eddie Turnbull, the hardest shot of his day, had ever been able to rectify in him. The other was that he did dither in clearing from hand and any forward who could manoeuvre him on to his weaker foot had him in trouble. There may have been a hint of poetic justice in this disallowal for in a league match at Parkhead, Lennox scored a goal in similar circumstances when almost all there were persuaded that he had used a hand in the scoring.

Celtic were livid and when Lennox came crashing down in the box without any recompense, Jimmy Johnstone became the second Parkhead man whose name was enquired for by

1970 ABERDEEN v. CELTIC. There may have been some doubt about the award of this Aberdeen penalty but Joe Harper was calmness itself. He left Celtic goalkeeper Evan Williams without the ghost of a chance with this perfectly-placed spot kick.

Bobby Davidson. Half-time came with Turnbull impressing on his side that they had done nothing yet. Celtic were come-back specialists par excellence and they would certainly throw everything at Aberdeen in the opening minutes of the second half. They did, but Clark, now considerably more chastened and alert, was equal to anything that came his way. McNeill had got a slight knock but the substitution that Celtic made was the crafty Auld for the more ramstam John Hughes.

The Aberdeen support sweated it out, it had been a long time since 1947. Seven minutes to go and the Cup seemed won. Derek McKay broke down the left, gave Jim Forrest the ball. The ex-Ranger shot, Williams parried and McKay who had started the move by turning Tommy Gemmell was there, however improbably, to squeeze in the rebound from a tight angle.

And that was that? It might have been against anyone else but Celtic. To their great credit on a day when they had not played well and decisions had consistently gone against them, they found a last source of energy and this time Lennox's goal was declared legitimate with just one minute of normal time to go. If any side could salvage a draw it was Celtic. They had done it against Motherwell in 1931. They had always been able to do it and would indeed manage to redeem a lost cause against Dundee United in the 80s. They threw everyone forward and here in the last analysis is why Aberdeen deserved to win. Conventional wisdom in a 2-1 situation with a minute to go says that "out the park wins matches" but Turnbull, screaming from the side, knew that Celtic would leave themselves dangerously bare at the back as they poured forward. So it proved, Joe Harper pushing a shrewd ball forward for his room-mate, Derek McKay, to leave Williams totally helpless.

The pandemonium persisted after the match, Aberdeen delighted as they had every right to be, Celtic disconsolate. Jock Stein congratulated Aberdeen with good grace but on the subject of the refereeing, he was almost incoherent with rage, though not so incoherent that he was not fined by the S.F.A. for expressing his considered opinion of it. More might have come from it but the looming return match with Leeds United had to be attended to and passions cool as quickly as they bubble in football.

In any case there had been other reasons for the Aber-

1970 ABERDEEN v. CELTIC. Cup hero Derek Mckay wins this ball in the air despite the close attentions of future Aberdeen manager Billy McNeill. Tommy Gemmell and Jim Brogan are the apprehensive onlookers.

deen victory. Throughout the ninety minutes they had chased, snapped and harried at the Celtic players, admirable tactics against a side which had such a fearsome reputation. More, their mental preparation for the game had been absolutely right. Jim Parkinson commented particularly on this in the *Glasgow Herald:*

"Aberdeen approached the electric tension of the big occasion at Hampden with the nonchalance of boys going on a picnic outing and they maintained a relaxed mental state throughout the game."

That was a fair assessment and it should not be over-looked that Aberdeen had scored three times against the best team not only in Scotland but in Britain and in 1969-70, Benfica were the only other team to do that. Football can be the hardest of task-masters and it would have been foolish not to have enjoyed the moment when it presented itself. Aberdeen did not fall into that error.

Aberdeen went back north. The Yank at Gleneagles was as good as his word and threw the most lavish of parties for the returning victors. As the bus went north on the Sunday morning, the day on which Eddie Turnbull was 47, groups of people stood at the roadside waving with fixed, pleased grins. The Provost of Stonehaven clambered aboard the coach to pass on the good wishes and congratulations of his fellow citizens.

When eventually the party reached Aberdeen they transferred to an open-top coach at Bridge of Dee. Through choked streets they passed, the players taking it in turn to display the Cup with boyish enthusiasm. And some of them were boys, there had been no younger captain of a Cup-winning team than Martin Buchan, and Arthur Graham had scarcely five months before been playing in the obscurity of Junior football with Cambuslang Rangers in the Central League.

The celebrations were extended and heart-felt but not so excessive as to prevent Aberdeen recording a victory over Hibernian at Easter Road on the Monday night, perhaps the single most remarkable thing about the whole weekend. It had been a notable performance and a reward for the unremitting slog of Eddie Turnbull who was sometimes difficult, not infrequently impossible, but whose irascible nature did not conceal a real concern for his players and a deep knowledge of and instinct for the game. It is remarkable how many players who

After 23 years the Cup is back at Pittodrie and the board rejoices.

served in their time under several managers will say on reflection, "Ned Turnbull was the best of them".

Football is always a better game when it can give credit to the opposition. It was good that Aberdeen had won, monopoly from whatever quarter it comes is damaging to the public and this holds true in sport. Nevertheless, Celtic's immediate response was totally admirable in that they hauled themselves up from the depths of disappointment and completed the double against Leeds United in the return at Hampden Park. The 134,000 who went to the game — 7,000 more than had witnessed the now-legendary Real Madrid-Eintracht final in 1960 — saw a John Hughes who was as devastating in mid-week as he had been ineffectual on the Saturday. Yet some of the damage inflicted by Aberdeen seemed to linger. Celtic would win many more championships but April 1970 could truthfully be said to have marked the absolute zenith of their wonderful spell. They disposed of Leeds United but then lost to Feyenoord in a European Cup final which they were as strong favourites to win as they had been underdogs in 1967 against Inter Milan.

For Aberdeen with a young, talented side, it should have been the beginning of a Golden Age but in those days a provincial side was never more vulnerable than at the moment of success. On reflection, that is probably equally true, perhaps even more so, as football moves into the 1990s. Martin Buchan went to Manchester United where he was deeply influential. Pedigree is important in football though no guarantee of success and his father, likewise Martin, had been a gifted player during his short time with Aberdeen.

Joe Harper went off to Everton and although he would be back, it is seldom that club affiliation, unlike love, is more wonderful the second time around. The supporter can only speculate ruefully as to what Aberdeen might have managed had his service to the club been unbroken. The enormously talented Arthur Graham gave good and long service before joining a Leeds United side which by 1977 had lost most of their considerable ability, but none of their less-endearing habits. By the time Graham went there, they were a shadow of the extremely able, if also extremely cynical side that they had been.

It tends to be forgotten that Bobby Clark, now seen as a Pittodrie fixture, would have been away too if Stoke City had not reneged upon a previously-agreed figure so that the big keeper remained at Pittodrie to the delight of the supporters for many seasons. In doing so, he saw off every challenger for his position, and some of those challengers were internationalists in their own right.

And what of Derek McKay? The dreamer of dreams, he who had been certain of victory, vanished as dramatically as he had come, in a rocket-like flight. He brought to mind a phrase of Burns,

"Or like the Borealis race
  That flit ere ye can point their place."

There was to be no headlining English transfer for this callant from Macduff with astonishingly direct ideas on how the game should be played. Within months rather than years, he had said farewell to Scottish football but he had won on the field in a similarly brief period what some Aberdeen stars of the past had wrought a score of years to achieve and never managed.

On that afternoon in 1970 as the crowds frothed in the streets of Aberdeen, as the players made in-jokes to each other and in turn held the Cup aloft exultantly, it was enough that fathers could show the spectacle to their small sons and in so doing remember what their fathers had told them about 1947 — the previous great day.

1970 — BOBBY CLARK REMEMBERS

The final of 1970 was my second with the Dons, I'd already been at Hampden for the 1967 game with Celtic. What I remember about that one was that for half an hour I was the only man in the Aberdeen dressing-room. The bus got lost but of course I didn't know that and I almost began to wonder if I hadn't turned up on the wrong day! As Jimmy Wilson told you, we missed Eddie Turnbull terribly on the day. He was an astonishing coach, indeed when I turned professional, I decided to go to Aberdeen because he would be there. He could have a tremendous effect on a side at half-time and his talks then were capable of transforming a game, I've seen it happen many a time.

Of the 1967 game I only remember in detail their second goal, scored by Willie Wallace. I learned a lesson from it, not to come too far off my near post. Jimmy Johnstone saw me come, slipped it to Wallace who had a lot of goal to shoot at. If I'd stayed on the line I'd have reduced the target for Willie.

1970 was a great match and I think we really won it with our victory at Parkhead in the League on the previous Monday. It was a great win, quite comfortable really, and Eddie Turnbull brought it off without tipping his hand for the final. Jocky Scott was outstanding though he didn't make the final but young Arthur Graham, who played his first game that night, did. Some of us had a lot to prove. I was just back in the side after a year of being reserve to Ernie McGarr. We hadn't always played well in the run-up to the final. We had been dismal against Clydebank in a match at Pittodrie, so bad that the crowd ended by cheering Clydebank, I think it may have been Martin Buchan's first match as skipper.

We had tremendous team spirit however and this was shown in a later round at Brockville when we had to field a much-weakened team because of 'flu. We had five or six players out. I think it was that day that we realised what a potentially dangerous player Derek McKay could be. I really think that on the day at Hampden, Jock Stein was out-guessed by Eddie Turnbull, and that is a remarkable statement to make, I know.

Of the incidents that marked the game, I can say categorically that Bobby Lennox handled the ball when he dispossessed me. What is ironical is that in a League match at Parkhead he had done the same thing far less skilfully — we were both standing still at the time in that match — and yet the goal had been awarded then, an absolutely outrageous decision. In the Cup Final it was harder to notice because we were both on the move, but Bobby Davidson, the referee, spotted it.

About the Celtic claim for a penalty, well, I would have found it quite hard to argue against, had a penalty been given for Martin Buchan's tackle on Bobby Lennox. But it wasn't and that's how it goes. We thought we were there when Derek McKay scored the second but immediately Bobby Lennox struck back and we were then much more nervous than when we had been ahead at 1-0, even although there were only a couple of minutes to go. I don't know that there was any great conscious decision to attack in the dying seconds, you don't write scripts for the closing stages of Cup finals. I think it was just that quite a few of our side had definite plans to take the Cup. Certainly at 2-1 there was a momentary tinge of panic.

They were a great side of course. Billy McNeill was a tremendously dominating force in the middle, always bearing down on the opposition. Tommy Gemmell too was a marvellously cavalier left-back, for ever pressing forward, although part of our tactical plan that day was to lure him forward and then pitch the ball in behind him for Derek McKay. We had plenty of pace up front for Jim Forrest was very speedy and young Arthur Graham wasn't exactly a slouch. Bobby Lennox too was an outstanding player, always totally unready to admit that any game was lost. We had to beat that day one of the best sides in Europe after all. In the 1967 final, Jimmy Johnstone had destroyed us by coming through the middle. This time, we double-marked him, George Murray and Martin Buchan mostly, and this slowed him down although, of course, you could never entirely eliminate the danger from Jimmy.

Jock Stein, although angry at a couple of refereeing decisions, was magnificent towards us as players after the match. It's odd how disorganised Cup finals sometimes get, I don't think that Aberdeen that day had either ribbons to tie round the Cup or champagne to celebrate the win. But Stein himself brought the Celtic champagne into our dressing room and when you think that nobody likes to lose a Cup final, you have to say that his action showed a touch of class.

Looking back I think the team changes in the early spring of 1970 may have been a last gamble by Eddie Turnbull.

They came off, largely because the players had a terrific team spirit at that time and were not going to make concessions to anyone. We had the satisfaction of knowing that in the Cup final, we had played just as well as we possibly could and that we had beaten a great side in Celtic.

CHAPTER EIGHT

1978 v. RANGERS

THE GREAT FREEZE

The thing that a manager dreads above all others is that his side will fail to produce form on the day when it matters. Defeat is hard to thole at any time, but slightly more palatable when it is felt that at least the team played to its potential and was simply beaten by a better side. This was to be the case in Aberdeen's next Scottish Cup appearance in 1978 when there took place what would only be called a collective failure of nerve.

Despite the long gap of eight years since the Dons had last appeared at Hampden, there were two survivors in their side from that day, Bobby Clark and, in his second incarnation, Joe Harper. Joe was to spend much time and energy in trying to secure Room 505 at the Excelsior Hotel, Glasgow, the room which he had occupied on the occasion of the great triumph of 1970. The manager, Billy McNeill, was new but with an involvement with Scottish Cup finals as a player that ran into double figures, he could reasonably claim to know more about them than anyone else in Scotland.

After a tentative start to the season and a catastrophic night at Ibrox where a 6-1 defeat banished any thoughts of the League Cup, the Dons took up the challenge to Rangers from a faltering Celtic, a team which now in Stein's last year at Parkhead was a parody of its former powerful and sublimely attractive self. Twenty-three undefeated league matches in a row up to the final was enough to push Rangers to the very last day of the season at Easter Road but not quite enough to redeem totally a self-imposed handicap. Nevertheless, in any run like that, a team acquires the habit and expectation of winning. The manager already had it, how could it be otherwise with his background, and he was well on the way to imparting this confidence to his team.

The passage through the various rounds of the Cup had been unremarkable, and matters had started with Ayr United being removed by an undramatic but professional 2-0 score line at Pittodrie. Home advantage again in the fourth round saw St Johnstone comfortably bested by three goals at Pittodrie and Aberdeen had no remote grounds for complaint when the quarter-finals found them due to receive Morton. They could only draw 2-2 at Pittodrie, however, to a Morton side that included the highly-individual Andy Ritchie and they were not a racing certainty by any means to survive the replay at Cappielow. A John McMaster penalty and an Ian Fleming goal took them through — just — and set up the oddity whereby in the semi-final against Partick Thistle at Hampden, Aberdeen played to their lowest crowd of the tournament with the exception of the Ayr match. Only 12,000 thought it worthwhile to go out to Mount Florida to see Aberdeen win 4-2, in the process of which Ian Fleming knocked three goals past Scotland goalkeeper, Alan Rough.

Rangers too had looked far from inevitable winners from the opening round. They had struggled hard at Berwick, an ill-omened ground for them, and Stirling Albion went away from Ibrox losers only by virtue of a single goal. Noticeably though, Rangers were getting stronger as the tournament progressed and victories over Kilmarnock and Dundee United were more emphatic.

There was indeed much to play for from the Rangers point of view. Their manager, Jock Wallace, was going for his second treble and no previous Rangers manager had accomplished that. The gravel-voiced Wallace would bring to the line a team finely trained and honed. The forward line might be lacking in physique but it contained several players of outstanding ability. The critics had initially been quick to scoff at Wallace's Foreign Legion style training on the sands of Gullane but they equally quickly had to concede that this "drill sergeant" was completing the recovery of self-esteem begun by Willie Waddell. For ten years after 1965 Rangers had done little else but react to whatever plans Jock Stein had concocted. That had changed, they would now set trends, they would now initiate policy. That was potentially ominous for Aberdeen.

There was enough talent in the Aberdeen side for Billy McNeill to await the outcome of events with justifiable confidence. Bobby Clark in goal had been a Don for over thirteen years and at that moment was the most capped Aberdeen player ever. He had just been selected for the Scottish party for Argentina which would be under the World Cup charge of Alistair McLeod, a former Aberdeen manager and an unsurpassed enthuser of footballers. Clark would be joined in the party by the wearer of the number 2 jersey, Stuart Kennedy, who in the fashion of modern wide defenders often appeared more like the traditional winger as he raced down the flank to attack. Across the field, the choice of his partner came as rather a surprise, Steve Ritchie from Hereford not appearing with Aberdeen until the semi-final tie and even then being substituted in the match. He always gave the impression of being just a little in water that was too deep but he retained his place for the final in place of competition from Chic McLelland.

Next name on the team-sheet was John McMaster who bid fair to become one of the most famous Pittodrie players of all time but severe injury would ensure that he did not. The powerful Willie Garner would seal off the middle and a young man, Willie Miller, still short in service and far from the folklore status which he eventually attained but impressive enough already to be captain, completed what aged reporters delight to call "the mid-line". Dom Sullivan — no-one ever called him Dominic — had been brought up north by Billy McNeill who remembered him from when both had been with Clyde. Ian Fleming had given abundant proof in the semi-final that given half a chance he could profit from it and Joe Harper's place was secure as the club's record scorer in all its history. A little tubbier, perhaps a shade less cobra-like in the box, he was still a man to be neglected at the opposition's peril.

Drew Jarvie had a special motivation for the big day. As a Junior with Kilsyth Rangers he had missed the Scottish Cup Final in 1967 and although given a compensatory medal he would have agreed with the renowned Willie Cooper of 1947 that it wasn't the same thing at all. Nevertheless he was in with a chance of completing a most rare treble since as an amateur he had won a Scottish Cup medal with Kirkstyle Thistle. He expressed well the professional's need to win things rather than just to play attractively:

"We have had a great season but we have not won anything. If we don't beat Rangers then people will look at the record books and what they see there will not tell them how good we have been." The Ibrox defence need hold no terrors for him for in the course of the season he had scored five times in six matches against Rangers.

Finally Duncan Davidson on the left had the manager-pleasing trait of making straight for goal and of having a shot, if nothing else immediately appeared to present itself. Of the fringe players, the recently signed Ian Scanlon from Notts County had created a very good impression on the last day of the season in a drawn match at Easter Road and would come very close to selection for the final itself. The two most promising youngsters at Pittodrie were missing. Steve Archibald was ineligible and Gordon Strachan was not selected.

Billy McNeill, at the end of his first season with the club, gave it an unusual managerial accolade: "It's been fun, hasn't it?" He had already decided that there would be no special build-up for the game, it would be business as usual; "We will prepare as we have done all season and we haven't done too badly out of it."

Rangers had spent the last few days preparing at Largs. Jock Wallace had at his disposal an ideal mixture of strength and subtlety. The goalkeeper was the 6'4" tall Peter McCloy, the "Girvan Lighthouse", who had seemingly been keeping goal since the days of string-collared jerseys. There was tremendous experience too in the persons of Sandy Jardine and John Greig. Alone of that Rangers team the latter had known the long years of subordination to Celtic. He had soldiered on loyally and good-humouredly through the dark days and now found himself on the verge of winning the treble for a third time. No-one else, not even Jock Stein, had succeeded in doing that.

Tom Forsyth, acquired by Rangers from Motherwell, had a cheerful off-field presence that belied his fearsome tackling on it. The big Aberdonian, Colin Jackson, was given to leaving his defensive beat to inflict damage on opposing defences at free kicks and corners while there were few to equal Alex MacDonald in his ability to switch the point of attack with a cross-field pass. It was up front that Rangers, to the dispassionate onlooker, appeared to have a considerable advantage. Tommy McLean was the only one of three brothers still playing. Jim was in charge at Tannadice and Willie had managed various clubs. The little ex-Kilmarnock winger was a deadly and precise user of the stationary ball at set pieces while in open play he could float a ball to the head of an unattended colleague. Inside him was a first-season senior, Bobby Russell, whom Jock Wallace in a comparison of marvellous percipience described as another edition of the great Jimmy Mason of Third Lanark. After the match he was to make another highly flattering allusion when he compared Russell with the brilliant John White of Tottenham Hotspur. Russell was the type of creative inside-forward which seemed to have vanished from the Scottish game and it was perhaps significant that he had taken the once traditional but now rare path of ascent from Junior football.

The only person of imposing physical stature in the Rangers attack was Derek Johnstone. Throughout his career he dithered between being an old-fashioned centre-forward or a central defender but his divided ambitions did not prevent his becoming the leading scorer in the Premier League. Another former Kilmarnock player, Gordon Smith, was fast over the ground and skilful with it and on the left there was the enigmatic but prodigiously gifted Davie Cooper.

Cooper could be an irritation to his supporters, for there were not infrequent occasions on which the game seemed no more than a passing distraction to him. He could go past a man at will when in the humour, his corner kicks swerved wickedly and his free kicks were both venomous and intelligent. With Cooper in the side, any free kick within a range of 30 yards was little inferior in danger to the award of a penalty kick.

Both camps had sweated blood during the previous week because several leading players had accumulated bookings and lay under threat of suspension. In the event, Derek Parlane of Rangers fell foul of the magistrates of Park Gardens but Alex MacDonald and Doug Rougvie won reprieves although the latter was not required by Aberdeen. Brian McGinley acted as referee.

By this time the build-up to the Cup Final in so far as it affected spectators lacked much of the cheerful good-humour which had made the day such a great social occasion. No longer did large numbers of Aberdonians roam the streets of Glasgow; now many of the Dons' followers would never have the occasion to see the city centre. Their special trains were routed to the neighbouring King's Park station and supporters' buses came by carefully mapped-out directions to the surroundings of the ground itself. As a reminder of persistent bad crowd behaviour in recent years, the Cup Final tickets themselves bore warning notices about the introduction to the ground of alcohol and cautioned severely against its misuse.

These then were the players destined to participate in the Scottish Cup Final of 1978.

ABERDEEN: Clark; Kennedy, Ritchie, McMaster, Garner, Miller, Sullivan, Fleming, Harper, Jarvie, Davidson.

RANGERS: McCloy; Jardine, Greig, Forsyth, Jackson, MacDonald, McLean, Russell, Johnstone, Smith, Cooper.

Speaking on the eve of the game, Billy McNeill had been all too prophetic as he talked of his anxieties:

"My only slight worry for tomorrow is how quickly they will settle. Of course they will be nervous. I was nervous before my LAST Cup Final and I played in a few."

Independently, Bobby Clark, a veteran at 32, said much the same thing. "My first final was 11 years ago and I wasn't in the least nervous then, in fact I spent the day before learning to canoe on Loch Lomond. You probably get more perturbed as you get older."

Whatever the rights of it, young and old Aberdeen players did not get over a bad attack of nerves which lasted for the entire ninety minutes. There was not a single Don, combing his hair in the dressing room after the match, who could have looked in the mirror and in honesty said: "Well, we lost, but I could not have played any better."

The scoreline will go down as Aberdeen 1, Rangers 2, but it is grossly misleading if the impression taken from it is that the game was close. In every art of the game Rangers were streets ahead, thanks largely to the scheming Russell who dispatched a constant stream of through passes like so many

1978 ABERDEEN v. RANGERS. Bobby Clark is left stranded as Alex MacDonald gets the faintest of touches to a right wing cross to give Rangers a first-half lead.

stiletti. He was the virtually unanimous selection as Player of the Match and with Gordon Smith he saw to it that Aberdeen were quietly and expertly throttled in mid-field.

Aberdeen played that day as if their feet were encased in diving boots. They lost two bad goals and seemed at no time capable of rallying. The first goal came when McLean pitched over a cross from the right and Alex MacDonald made considerable ground to score with a glancing header. Full marks to the Ranger but it has to be said that Bobby Clark's effort to save — half-stranded as he was between goal-line and penalty spot — carried very little conviction.

For a while in the second half, Rangers could not make their total domination count and there was always the outside chance that Aberdeen might snatch an equaliser, hang on and take the tie to a replay in which they could not possibly play so badly again. That faint hope was snuffed out, almost laughably, by Rangers' second goal. It was not exactly a secret that Derek Johnstone was extremely good in the air, his headers were known to have both power and direction. It was angering, therefore, to see him the target of a Tommy McLean cross and realise that the big centre-forward was rising to it totally unchallenged. There was not an Aberdeen defender within yards as Johnstone directed a header which was so accurately placed that Bobby Clark was denied even the consolation of a despairing dive, being left firm-footed as the ball flashed to the back of the net.

So inept were Aberdeen on the day that if they were to score it would require something freakish and sure enough the goal they got with five minutes to go was one of the greatest Final flukes ever. Steve Ritchie had pressed forward and, up with his attackers, half-hit, half-scooped a shot from six yards. The ball rose almost vertically like a water spout, drifted forward a little, came down on the goal-line and a weird forward spin took it up into the roof of the net just behind the cross-bar. So convinced was Peter McCloy that the ball was going over that at the actual moment when the ball crossed the line, he was swinging nonchalantly on his cross-bar.

Five minutes remained and Aberdeen had been thrown a totally unexpected lifeline. The question now was, could they salvage anything from this game, and the answer was that they could not. In a potentially exciting situation they never remotely threatened Rangers' goal again and when the whistle came the Dons could not leave the field quickly enough. They had won entry to the European Cup Winners Cup anyway by reason of Rangers having also won the League but for the moment that was comparatively little solace.

Back in Aberdeen next morning, the players dispiritedly prepared for a tour of the city, fearing that their reception by the supporters would be at best lukewarm, at worst actively hostile. They knew that they had let the fans down badly. In the event, the response was astonishing. Thousands of supporters, cheering vigorously, lined the city streets and there were certainly 10,000 inside Pittodrie. From the vigour of their applause it became evident that they were not prepared to let one bad performance — even one very bad performance — stand in the way of an excellent season's work.

Players and manager pledged themselves to do better next season, their spines visibly straightening in the warmth of their welcome. What had been a wearisome chore for subdued and embarrassed players was become a happy event. Billy McNeill grabbed a microphone and eventually the clamouring crowd was still. He thanked them and promised them future compensation:

" It's hard to have been so close and to have had to settle for nothing. We were very disappointed yesterday but today you have made it a lot better. We have made a resolution to give you something next year."

What the fans got next year was a new manager. In an astonishing chain of events within days of the Scottish Cup Final, the triumphant Rangers manager, Jock Wallace, twice winner of the treble, had resigned in circumstances which have never to this day been fully explained. His successor would be that paragon of club servants, John Greig. This posed a threat to a Celtic side which had just had comfortably their least productive season in 12 years. There was a feeling that the time had come for Jock Stein to step aside but who on earth was capable of succeeding someone with Stein's record at home and European level?

Celtic thought that his lieutenant, his captain rather, Billy McNeill, might be well up to the job and invited him to try. McNeill was confronted with a genuine dilemma. He had been made very welcome at Aberdeen and by any standards of

1978 ABERDEEN v. RANGERS. Dom Sullivan and Billy McNeill, who would later join up again at Parkhead, draw considerable comfort from the massed Aberdeen fans the morning after the match.

1978 ABERDEEN v. RANGERS. WE'LL SUPPORT YOU EVERMORE. The fact that Aberdeen have just been beaten 2-1 in the Scottish Cup Final by Rangers makes no difference at all to these two young admirers of Pittodrie hero Joe Harper.

fairness his first season there had been successful and better, extremely promising for the future. In Gordon Strachan, Ian Scanlon and Steve Archibald, he had made three signings whose subsequent careers would enable any manager to warm his hands at the fire of his own judgement.

More than that, McNeill liked the North-East and saw it as a very desirable place in which to bring up a young family and his wife's enthusiasm for the area was greater still. Aberdeen had given the ex-Celtic captain the chance to manage at top level and he was very conscious of this. In his playing days, however, he had been a one-club man and that club had been Celtic. If the offer to manage them had come earlier than he would ideally have wished, it still had to be considered very carefully because, if rejected once, there might well be no second asking.

The lure of Parkhead proved too strong and Billy McNeill went south with the regrets and best wishes of the Aberdeen directors. It seemed as if the greater economic power of the two big Glasgow clubs would prevail again as it always had done. The sense of disappointment in Aberdeen perhaps caused the selection of Alex Ferguson of St Mirren as the next man in charge to lose something of the impact it would have made in happier circumstances. It should not have done. Aberdeen found themselves a manager who was convinced that he had the necessary qualities for success in the top flight and that any team managed by himself must for that reason start as favourites in any competition for which they were entered. Under his tempestuous leadership, Aberdeen would become one of the great powers in Scottish football in the 1980s. The three major trophies would fall to them, they would become the third Scottish club to take a European trophy and in the matter of the Scottish Cup in particular, success in that competition would become as regular and frequent as failure to take it had been hitherto.

And in the young man Miller, the number six, moving quietly and without fuss to his appointed tasks, Ferguson had "the keystane o' the brig'" and the man round whom would be built the successful and exhilarating Aberdeen side of the 1980s. Those fans who cheered lustily in defeat at Pittodrie on that Sunday afternoon of defeat undoubtedly did better than they knew.

Meanwhile, a million miles away from the glare of publicity, Derek McKay, whose wanderings had taken him since 1970 to South Africa, Hong Kong and Australia, found himself on the Ross County open to transfer list. He had failed to report for a home match against Keith but you had to look very hard to find the relevant paragraph.

1978 — BOBBY CLARK REMEMBERS

This was for me the most disappointing final of the three I played in for Aberdeen. The first one in 1967 I was a part-timer and quite relaxed, after all if I'd played for a team like Clyde, the car mechanics would have repaired and the teachers taught in the run-up to the game, and of course with Queen's Park, all the players had been part-timers. The second final in 1970, well of course we had a famous win. But we never got going at all in 1978.

We'd no great reason to be nervous playing Rangers and that doesn't take anything away from them. We had just gone through a spell of 23 games without defeat and of six previous meetings with Rangers that season, we had won four of them. We just picked a one-off game to have a collective stinker.

I wasn't too happy with my own performance at the first goal. Wee Tommy McLean floated over a cross which I think he'd tell you now was really meant for Derek Johnstone. I started to come for it and had shifted my weight onto the front foot when Alex MacDonald stole in. He didn't get much on the ball, it was just a faint deflection, rather like an outside edge at cricket, but I had shifted my weight, and as you know, that's all it takes, a weight shift. If I had stayed at home I don't think the header would have presented me with much in the way of problems.

I am inclined to think that one of the reasons we lost was the fact that we had replaced Chic McLelland by Steve Ritchie shortly before the final. Chic could always put the peter on Tommy McLean, whose great strength was his ability to make space and get the crosses in. Chic could close him down very successfully and prevent him doing this but Steve Ritchie was a different type of player and on the day Tommy got a lot of scope. This was shown at the second goal when big Derek Johnstone was left all on his own in front of goal to meet a cross from the right. He took it flush in the middle of his forehead and I didn't even have time to move my feet before the ball was in the net and there was no way back really.

Don't misunderstand me when I say we had expected to win, Rangers were a very good side. They were very strong on the wings with McLean and Cooper, both great crossers of the ball, D.J. was knocking them in from the middle and young

Bobby Russell, a great user of the ball, was just beginning to make himself known.

We scored a weird goal with a few minutes to go. Steve Ritchie sent a ball straight up in the air and it dropped almost vertically below the crossbar, catching Peter McCloy out. A lot was said then about the Hampden Swirl but I've always taken that with a grain of salt and remember I played every other week there for more than three years when I was with Queen's. Winds blow just the same at several other grounds and I think this has only attached to Hampden because more big games are played there. I think that what happened that day was that Steve simply mis-hit the ball and this deceived Peter. A goalkeeper is always more liable to save a correctly-struck shot.

When Steve's shot went in, we thought for a moment "Hey, we can maybe get out of jail!" but even that did not seem able to inspire us and the match just petered out. I would certainly have liked to have another shot at that first goal! Billy McNeill was specially disappointed as we were for him. He had worked very hard with us. Eddie Turnbull was perhaps the better tactician but Billy was very good at encouraging players and giving them a good opinion of themselves. Both men were masterly in making training sessions interesting and never letting the tempo flag, I'm sure that that was something that Billy had largely picked up from Jock Stein. I would rate Eddie Turnbull alongside Stein as one of the two greatest Scottish soccer tacticians of my time — that's how good I thought he was.

CHAPTER NINE

1982 V. RANGERS

THE DONS OUTLAST THEM

W hen Aberdeen were given another chance against Rangers four years later, the most important change was not in playing personnel but in the managership. Alex Ferguson was a Govan lad and had all the fierce combativeness associated with that district of Glasgow. As a player, he had always been one for making opposing defences aware that he was part of the game. Johnny Graham, his team-mate at Ayr, described him thus: "He was always in the penalty area, always up for the chance and he took a lot of abuse." Benny Rooney, who remembered him from his St Johnstone days, described him as having "the sharpest elbows in the game".

His Ibrox period had not been his happiest or most productive. That had come at Dunfermline where he had scored 46 goals in 51 games and yet found himself left out of the Cup Final side of 1965 against Celtic. It was a bitter blow at the time but it made him realise vividly the pain that a player feels when omitted on the big day and it was to be a useful experience for him as a manager although, despite his abrasive image, it was something he never found easy to do.

The 1982 Cup Final took place before the back-drop of the Falklands War which threatened to stop Scottish participation in the forthcoming World Cup in Spain. The Scottish Professional Footballers' Association felt that it would be inappropriate to take part in a competition where Argentina were the Cup-holders and advocated withdrawal. Their view was not shared by the Secretary of the Scottish Football Association, Ernie Walker, who robustly dismissed it as "irresponsible nonsense". In the event the Home Countries participated but it was a strange enough situation in all conscience, not exactly a state of war but something very like it. The resolution of the situation was good news for Jim Leighton, Stuart Kennedy, Alex McLeish and Willie Miller who had all been selected for Scotland.

On the basis of the season's work up until then, Aberdeen started clear favourites for the final, not that this would necessarily mean very much on the day. A poll of Premier Division managers came out solidly for the Dons who had certainly had the harder passage to the final. It had begun with a tricky visit to Motherwell which a John Hewitt goal had seen safely negotiated and then in the fourth round, Celtic, always likely winners, were sent to Pittodrie. Again Hewitt did his stuff with a solitary goal and in the next round two Gordon Strachan penalties were highly influential in disposing of Kilmarnock 4-2. The semi-final required two games against St Mirren who succumbed by 3-2 after a 1-1 draw, Saints keeper Billy Thomson having a most unhappy night.

Rangers' progress had not been awe-inspiring. In the first two rounds, they got rid of Albion Rovers and Dumbarton as they would have been expected to do, in a most tradesman-like manner, it should be said, and then had a good win of 2-0 over Dundee. Their semi-final against Forfar Athletic at Hampden was supposed to be something of a formality, but turned out to be far from that. Forfar took the honours in a goalless draw and had a very credible penalty claim turned down in the last minute. Even in the replay, they kept Rangers at bay for an hour until in the end superior fitness told.

Aberdeen had done well in the League too and went into the last day with an outside chance of winning the title. For that to happen, they had to beat Rangers at Pittodrie and hope that Celtic would lose at home to St Mirren. No-one could say that the Dons did not give it their best shot for when the half-time whistle went, they were four goals to the good and as yet there was no scoring at Parkhead. It looked as if Rangers might well be in for the drubbing of all time but in football heavy scoring is seldom sustained throughout the entire ninety minutes. Celtic's first goal, scored by McCluskey, took 63 minutes to arrive but it was followed by two others from McAdam and the previous scorer and the green and whites were champions. In explaining the second half, Alex Ferguson said:

"We were waiting for the cheer from the terracing which should tell us that St Mirren had scored but it never came and after that the impetus left us."

The League therefore had slipped away but such an emphatic victory would do nothing for morale in the Rangers dressing room. It was true that Sandy Jardine had to go off injured after 13 minutes and had been replaced by Tommy McLean, a change that owed more to necessity than any particular tactical thinking, but Colin Jackson had put through his own goal and John Hewitt had rattled in a hat-trick. Aberdeen would approach the final in buoyant mood, and they would make a light preparation at Cruden Bay Golf Club.

It would not have been a Cup final had there been no last-minute scares about injury and unavailability. In this department Rangers came out worst. Most importantly for them, Derek Johnstone would not play, an absence which was all the more exasperating because his injury had been sustained in a Testimonial Match for Sandy Jardine at Ibrox, giving pith to the old saw that it is the "funny games" that are the most dangerous. Ian Redford would also sit out the final and these two men were considerable losses. Aberdeen hearts had sunk when in a League match at Paisley ten days before, Gordon Strachan had sustained a broken nose against St Mirren, but it would take more than that to make the little red-haired inside man miss his first Scottish Cup Final. Peter Weir, however, the long-striding winger acquired from St Mirren, would not be fit enough to turn out and his ability to send over curving crosses which drew the keeper from his line would certainly be missed. These were the men who made it to the starting line.

ABERDEEN: Leighton; Kennedy, Rougvie, McMaster, McLeish, Miller, Simpson, McGhee, Strachan, Cooper, Hewitt. Substitutes: Bell, Black

RANGERS: Stewart; Jardine (McAdam), Dawson,

McClelland, Jackson, Bett, Cooper, Russell, Dalziel (McLean), Miller, MacDonald. Substitutes: McAdam, McLean

All the Aberdeen survivors in the Aberdeen side from 1978, Kennedy, McMaster and Miller, were in defence. Of the rest, Jim Leighton would shortly follow his predecessor Bobby Clark into the Scottish goal, while Doug Rougvie was burning to avenge what he considered an unjust sending off against Rangers in a League Cup final some years before. Alex McLeish in the centre defence appeared awkward and gangling until one began to notice how little ever got past him. It was all change up front. Gordon Strachan had come from Dundee and was a manager's ideal, a skilful player who nevertheless did not expect the ball to be delivered to him by conveyor belt but was perfectly prepared to go out and challenge for it. Neil Simpson was London-born but had come to Pittodrie as an exotically-named Middlefield Wasp, his powerful build was perhaps only surpassed by that daunting man-boy, Neale Cooper, who at the tender age of 18 resembled a Sherman tank with legs.

Mark McGhee had also arrived from England, from Newcastle United, where he had failed to dazzle. He would have achieved a great deal by the time he went back to them from Parkhead. Finally, John Hewitt's frequent goal-scoring successes were all the more acceptable because he had more or less grown up within the shadow of Pittodrie. It could well be said that his successes were all the more meritorious because life is harder for the local boy, Harry Yorston from an earlier age could well have testified feelingly to that. It was a young Aberdeen side but tempered in the furnace of matches against such as Liverpool, Eintracht, Frankfurt, Ipswich Town and Hamburg.

The Rangers side was liberally supplied with men who could have worn a Scottish Cup medal on their watchchains, had such accessories still been fashionable. Goalkeeper Jim Stewart had wasted no time in acquiring a medal, owning one in the first season following his transfer from Middlesbrough. The men in front of him, Sandy Jardine and Alistair Dawson, had walked up to the presentation dais on that same Wednesday night of 1981. Rangers had made some good signings at that time, none better than the Northern Ireland international, John McClelland, who was an inspiring captain and lethal at the near post whenever there was a long throw-in or a corner. He would bear watching. Colin Jackson's reputation was secure and Jim Bett had obviously benefited from his early spell in Europe. He KNEW that work rate and running about daft were not necessarily the same thing.

For the rest, Aberdeen knew all about Cooper and Russell although Gordon Dalziel remained to be worked out. A surprise in the Ibrox team was the inclusion of the veteran Alex Miller and the team was completed by the immensely-promising John MacDonald who seemed meant to take his place with those other massive goal scorers for Rangers, Jim Forrest, Willie Thornton and Colin Stein, but somehow never did.

Alex Ferguson allowed just a noticeable trace of misgiving to surface in his pre-match comment:

"I've absolutely no fears whatever about this game, that is, no logical fears. The only thing is that a final is a final and anything can happen on the day."

He was relying on the experience of his four World Cup men to get him through the first twenty minutes, although Willie Miller made the point that whatever players like Simpson, Cooper and Hewitt might need, it was certainly not nursemaids. The game started quietly enough, there was a lot of midfield sparring, both sides were feeling each other out. A Strachan free kick saw McLeish head inches over, the big fellow would be difficult for the Rangers defence to pick up. Strachan was in the mood and he was illegally stopped by Jim Bett, an illegality which led to the taking of the Ranger's name.

When things appeared to be going eminently satisfactorily for the Dons, Rangers opened the scoring with fifteen minutes played and it was an excellent goal. Cooper set up Miller who fed Dalziel who had wandered out to the right. The young striker sent over a shoulder-high cross and John MacDonald had merely to stoop and let his head make the necessary deflection. The ball raced to the net and Jim Leighton had lost a goal for which he needed to feel not the slightest tinge of self-reproach.

Rangers a goal up, the bulk of the not particularly large crowd — there were only 53,000 there — baying triumphantly, Aberdeen supporters could have been pardoned for expressing their belief that this was a script with which they had reached undue familiarity. It was going to be very important that

135

Aberdeen should get back on terms quickly, before half-time it that were at all possible.

Given that it was possible, not too many of the red-clad fans would have made a successful stab at the identity of the scorer. The goal came in the 33rd minute and this was how it happened. Following a Hewitt corner, a McMaster shot was blocked by Jim Bett and came out to Alex McLeish standing unattended at the edge of the penalty area. His floated half-lob, half-chip eluded the desperately back-pedalling Jim Stewart and the teams were on level terms. Aberdeen supporters praised the surpassing delicacy of the controlled lob which had brought them equality, Rangers supporters cursed the hapless Jim Stewart for having failed to keep out an eminently saveable shot. The neutral observer, assuming that such an animal existed, would almost certainly have said "A bit of both". McLeish clinched the argument by remarking laconically that he'd previously scored a goal just like it - in a training session at Cruden Bay!

Before half-time Doug Rougvie had been booked for a rattling tackle on Sandy Jardine, a tackle which was to have its effect on the match. When the teams reappeared for the second half, the score remaining at 1-1, it could be seen that Jardine was not among the Rangers players and that his place had been taken by Colin McAdam. The second half was a dreich affair and indeed almost the only incident to stay in the memory was the late save by Jim Leighton from a flashing Gordon Dalziel header which kept Aberdeen in with a chance, it was a magnificent stop by the Aberdeen keeper.

So then to extra time, and the usual scenes of managers out on the pitch, pounding fists into palms, making points which it is doubtful if drained and exhausted players are capable of understanding, no matter how pertinent the advice. Rangers made the one voluntary substitution left to them, Gordon Dalziel went off and on came the veteran but recently out of favour Tommy McLean. Dougie Bell came on for Aberdeen's John McMaster and John Hewitt made way for another young lion, Eric Black.

The extra thirty minutes provided one of the greatest victories in Aberdeen's history. It is always particularly difficult to get back on terms in extra time and therefore particular importance attaches to the scoring of the first goal. Gordon Strachan, who had moved wide to the right wing to accommodate the introduction of Dougie Bell, broke out on the flank and pitched a well-judged cross in behind John McClelland. On the blind side, Mark McGhee was flying in and Aberdeen were ahead, 2-1 was the score, there were 27 minutes to endure. The biggest error Aberdeen could make now was to fall back on a sterile defence of their lead and to their credit they did not yield to this very real temptation. They continued to press forward and were rewarded with only two minutes of the first part of extra time remaining.

The goal was a personal disaster for Rangers' Alex Miller. Going in to tackle Mark McGhee he slipped, fell awkwardly and lamed himself, so that McGhee walked past him unopposed, took it to the line, looked up, saw Strachan and, as coolly as if it were a five a side midweek bounce game at Pittodrie training, rolled the ball in front of the redhead for what most people thought must be the final goal. At the change-over, John Greig did what he could to lift the spirits of his players, but 3-1 down would have been an awesome task in any circumstances. It became greater because Alex Miller who had bravely refused all attempts to take him off was limping at less than half-capacity out on the Hampden field which after almost two hours play seemed like vast untenanted spaces to his toiling colleagues.

Long years of Aberdeen failure against Rangers had bred a certain scepticism in their fans but with only fifteen minutes to survive, they could not throw away a 3-1 lead against a team with ten men and a swinger. Could they? Not this time. There was only one goal in the second half but once again it came Aberdeen's way. Neale Cooper broke through the unguarded centre, unguarded because Rangers to their eternal credit were still trying to carry the game to Aberdeen as indeed they had to if they were to have any chance of saving matters. Cooper got away, Jim Stewart came rushing to the edge of his area in a despairing attempt to stop him. Then followed the conclusive proof that this particular Scottish Cup had been meant to go to Aberdeen all along. Cooper's shot rebounded from Stewart, hit Cooper on the chest and suddenly the big fellow, ball and all, was past the goalkeeper with an open goal looming and the certain insurance of a two-goal lead. Neale milked the situation for all it was worth, nudging the ball up to the goal-line before bulging the net with a venomous shot from all of twelve inches.

It was a great moment for the Cunarder-built 18 year old who had given proof of his astonishing physical maturity by playing 43 first team matches in the course of the season. One began to see what Willie Miller meant when he said that these youngsters did not need anybody to hold their hands.

For Miller himself, it was a joyous day as he now had the complete set of medals, League, League Cup and Scottish Cup. Ahead of him in the immediate future was the chance to operate on the greatest stage of all, the World Cup in Spain, where Scotland's opponents would include Russia and Brazil. And if he needed anything further in the way of a compliment, there was the report in the papers that Rangers, shattered by the extent and circumstances of their defeat, were contemplating putting in a bid for him.

Had Miller gone, the immediate future might well have been less successful for Aberdeen. Their supporters do not like players leaving at all when they have made a considerable reputation but it is just tholeable if they go south or to Europe. No Scottish provincial club can afford to transfer players consistently to either member of the Old Firm and remain credible with their own support.

But in Miller's case it did not happen and the more pedantic among the Aberdeen supporters were proudly pointing out that their side had won the first-ever Scottish Cup Final to go to extra time on the first match. It was a newly-created dispensation of which Aberdeen would avail themselves again in the two years which were to follow.

There may well have been a touch of the prophetic in the penalty-kick competition which the players organised at Pittodrie on the Sunday. Fergie joined in and caused great hilarity when Jim Leighton, with a fine disregard for his future career, saved his manager's effort from the spot.

A little later Leighton himself, concentrating as deeply as if it had been the Final itself, scored with an immaculately struck penalty. But who had ever heard of penalty kicks deciding a Scottish Cup Final?

1982 — WILLIE MILLER REMEMBERS

I suppose in a way I was lucky in getting the bad Scottish Cup Final over first, that was in 1978. We went in with high hopes, we had been undefeated in 23 matches on the trot but we didn't play. Billy McNeill wasn't a man to tie you down too strictly, he would encourage us to think at set pieces — "if it's on do it," was a great phrase of his.

The captaincy didn't affect me, even although I was only 23 at the time. I like captaining, and wouldn't have played any better if I hadn't been captain. When we got that weird Steve Ritchie goal — he actually mis-hit it — just for a moment we thought we might sneak a draw, you have to clutch at straws in such situations.

Worse than losing was Billy McNeill's decision to go to Celtic. We really looked as if we had a team that could begin to go places and it was all the more severe a blow coming so soon after the departure of Ally McLeod. I'd won my first medal with Ally, a League Cup medal, and he not only had the whole club but the whole town buzzing, you felt that with him you could do anything, although I think the senior players found some of his training methods strange. Two managers gone in the same number of years, it began to look as if Aberdeen was just a staging post on the way to better things. There was a terrible uncertainty when the two men went, we didn't know that Fergie would come or that he'd be as good as he was. Bertie Auld was also much in contention for the job at that time.

In the 1982 final against Rangers, the loss of an early goal was a blow, although it was a good enough goal. For once we had started positively and contained Rangers' opening surge, yet we were still behind. The Rangers crowd can be extremely intimidating at Hampden if you let it be. These are home games for them, after all. We felt that we had to be level by half-time and big Alex's lob put us there. He'd scored a goal just like that in Cruden Bay training a couple of days before and one of the boys had shouted at him "Big man, you'll never do that again in your life"

At the end of ninety minutes — Jim Leighton had saved well just before the end — the boss and Archie Knox came out. At such a time it wasn't so much a tactical talk as a knock down and lift you up job. Fergie usually took you to task and then

Archie would lift you back up. Usually Fergie would say one thing that was important. He was a very bold user of substitutes, I've seen him make a change after ten minutes and it wasn't through injury.

When we went ahead 2-1 in extra time, there was no signal from the bench to defend that lead. Alex Ferguson would never tell you to sit on a lead. We knew Rangers would have to come out and so would lay themselves open. They did and we scored two more.

After the final, Rangers made an approach for me and I had two telephone conversations with John Greig. The first one was just to hear what Rangers had to say and of course it was a good offer. The second was to thank him for the interest in me but to tell him that I had decided to stay and play out my career with Aberdeen. I genuinely thought then that that Aberdeen team had more chance of being successful than the Rangers team of the time and I suppose that the events of the next two or three seasons proved that my judgement was correct.

1982 Willie Miller takes the trophy to show it to the delighted Aberdeen support after Rangers had been overcome in extra time.

CHAPTER TEN

1983 V. RANGERS

TWO CUPS AND A DRESSING-DOWN

In the whole history of the Scottish Cup, there can hardly have
been half a dozen occasions when a member of the Old Firm was
involved in the final stage without being considered as the hot
favourite to win. This was however most definitely the case in
the Scottish Cup Final of 1983 when public opinion was almost
unanimous in declaring that Aberdeen would emerge triumphant from the Hampden Park meeting of the clubs.

Those who thought on these lines could bring plenty of
evidence to bear in support of their belief. Aberdeen had been
by far the better side in the League, had scored four goals at
Pittodrie against Rangers in the late spring and indeed had gone
into the last day of the season with an outside chance of taking
the title. It was true that for this to happen lots of ifs and buts
had to fall into place. Aberdeen themselves had to defeat
Hibernian at Pittodrie while hoping that Rangers would take
care of Celtic at Ibrox, and that nerves would get the better of
Dundee United who would be champions for the first time if
they managed to clear the final hurdle at Dens Park.

At half-time on that Saturday, there was an incredulous
buzz on the Pittodrie terracings. Aberdeen were fulfilling their
part of the bargain and were comfortably two ahead of Hiber-

nian, while down at Ibrox, Rangers were ahead by the same margin. Dundee United, having scored two early goals as well, had been hauled back to an uncomfortable 2-1 interval lead and all things were still possible. It did not work out as desired, it was asking a lot for that to happen. Dundee United managed to cling on for the second half and it would not have mattered had they not done so, since Celtic rattled in an improbable four second-half goals against Rangers, Charlie Nicholas signing off with a nonchalant brace of penalty kicks before going to try his fortune in England. No title then, but a definite superiority established over their opponents, Rangers, in the course of the League campaign.

And of course there had been a much greater distinction gained, for this was the season when Aberdeen became the third Scottish club to win a European trophy when the Cup Winners Cup was secured by a 2-1 win in Gothenburg over the most famous European side of all, Real Madrid. On a night of pouring rain, the Dons rose to unprecedented heights. They had gone ahead with an Eric Black goal in 14 minutes and to all intents and purposes, had dominated play thereafter. In a fugitive Real raid, Alex McLeish had been perceptibly short with a pass-back on the sodden surface to his goalkeeper, leaving Jim Leighton with very little option but to pull down Isidro in the penalty area. Juanito took the kick and scored with great self-assurance.

Aberdeen continued to have the better of things but the game moved into extra time and would now require a flash of brilliance or an unforced error if a conventional decision were to be reached. Gratifyingly, the winner was a well-worked goal which totally split the Spanish defence beyond any questioning. Mark McGhee got away down the left wing, looked up and saw a red jersey streaking towards the penalty box. Inside the jersey was John Hewitt, who had come on as substitute for the tiring Eric Black with four minutes of normal time remaining. Now McGhee delivered a measured cross and Hewitt's flying header sent the ball spinning into the net seconds before he himself aquaplaned along the drenched turf to join the ball. For the remaining nine minutes, the major Aberdeen worry was that an intensification of the downpour might bring about the abandonment of the match.

That did not happen and the Dons had won a major European competition. Alex Ferguson was ecstatic in his reaction to the triumph: "Now we are a name. We have brought this club to the forefront of European football and that is very satisfying. We are now a side to be reckoned with. Remember that the final was televised to 42 countries, so people will know all about Aberdeen today."

Aberdonians reacted in different ways. In Gothenburg, chairman Dick Donald wept tears of joy at seeing his beloved club established among the aristocracy of European football. Back home in Aberdeen, as the final whistle went, people poured on to the streets, drier streets than they were in Sweden. Within ten minutes, a deserted Union Street, which could have done duty for the famous self-mocking postcard entitled "Aberdeen on a flag day" could have served as a model for the other which showed the thoroughfare packed out, "Aberdeen during a house to house collection". Cars drove aimlessly but happily up and down, sounding their horns incessantly, and the victorious team suddenly acquired a royal supporter as the statue of King Edward VII was irreverently draped with club scarves and favours.

It was in a continuing happy frame of mind that the manager, accompanied by Mark McGhee, who had been his first big signing when he paid Newcastle United £65,000 for him in March 1979, took the Cup Winners Cup down to Aberdeen Harbour to meet the fans who had made the long sea voyage from Gothenburg on the ferry, St Clair. Another important psychological blow had been struck. Aberdeen, and indeed Dundee United, were currently highly regarded in Europe, whereas for the present the Old Firm were of small account.

There was yet another area in which the Pittodrie side held a considerable advantage. The Scottish international pool had just been announced and Aberdeen furnished it with six players, whereas only two would be required from Ibrox. If further proof were needed of the tilt towards the New Firm, the two North-East clubs provided ten players in all, as against the six called up from the two historic Glasgow teams.

In addition, there were strong indications that the end of an era was approaching at Ibrox. Derek Johnstone was not considered for a final place, and neither were Gregor Steven or Colin McAdam. In addition, the highly serviceable Ian Redford would be unavailable to John Greig because of suspension. Put

143

all that together and it was scarcely surprising that every Premier Division manager asked plumped for Aberdeen, with the exception of Jock Wallace of Motherwell and Alex MacDonald of Hearts, and in both those cases, traditional loyalties might understandably be thought to have over-ruled considered judgement.

Aberdeen's progress through the previous rounds had been unspectacular but impressive because there had been no easy ties. The cup run had started with an excellent 4-1 win against Hibernian at Easter Road and Weir, Simpson, Watson and McGhee all got on the score sheet, the kind of sharing-out that always pleases a manager. Fans like the heavy individual scorer, but managers are all too conscious that injury can cripple if too much reliance is placed on any one member of the playing staff. There were odd goal wins against Dundee at home and Partick Thistle away, Peter Weir getting the winner at Firhill. He played the crucial role too in the semi-final against Celtic at Hampden in what was described as a far too physical game. Neale Cooper, concussed, was taken off in 65 minutes and it was his replacement, Peter Weir, who came on to score the only goal.

So it would be Aberdeen in the final and there they would meet Rangers who had required a replay and a last-minute goal to dispose of St Mirren. Aberdeen had had a last-minute scare about the fitness of Doug Rougvie, but the big fellow was in his accustomed place as David Syme took charge of the following sides:

ABERDEEN: Leighton; Rougvie (Watson), McMaster, Cooper, McLeish, Miller, Strachan, Simpson, McGhee, Black, Weir (Hewitt)

RANGERS: McCloy; Dawson, McClelland, McPherson, Paterson, Bett, Cooper (Davies), McKinnon, Clark, Russell, MacDonald (Dalziel)

The crowd at 62,979 was not at all impressive when compared with the multitudes of previous years, but two points should be made. The first was that the capacity of Hampden Park was contracting with almost every year that passed and even at that, it was 10,000 up on the gate when the two clubs had met the previous year at the same stage in the competition.

In the Rangers side were several new faces from that day

twelve months previously. The veteran Peter McCloy was back in goal and Ally Dawson had swapped the number three for the number two shirt. There were two new central defenders in the enormously tall Dave McPherson, who had come through the Ibrox reserve sides, and Craig Paterson, recently signed from Hibernian. Up front was the bustling Sandy Clark, fetched back from West Ham United, and the sturdy but serviceable Dave McKinnon. The Rangers manager, John Greig, had thought about including the clever young inside forward, Billy Davies, from the start, but eventually decided on putting him on the bench.

John Greig had approached the final with his usual robust common sense: "I could spend a full week telling my players to watch this and that about Aberdeen, but it is what WE do on the day that will count. We must be positive and give them problems not spend our time worrying about what problems they may give us."

The game itself was a sad let-down although it did not begin as such. Aberdeen made a bubbly start and McCloy justified his recall as early as the fourth minute with a good save from Eric Black. Four minutes later, Doug Rougvie sent a looping header beyond his fingers but also just beyond the crossbar. In a quick Rangers counter-attack, Cooper was menacing and then Sandy Clark was deservedly booked for clattering into the Aberdeen keeper, Jim Leighton. There was a bad moment or two when it looked as if the keeper might have to go off, but he was able to continue after fairly prolonged treatment.

The game deteriorated, Rangers visibly gaining in confidence as the expected red blitz failed to materialise. Half time arrived scoreless, but with Bobby Russell and Jim Bett increasingly dominant in mid-field for Rangers. Within four minutes of the restart, Jim Leighton had saved very well from John MacDonald, and shortly afterwards Aberdeen claimed in vain that Ally Dawson had armed the ball in effecting a clearance. Billy Davies came on as a Rangers substitute and before too long had the ball in the Aberdeen net, but he had very obviously fouled Neale Cooper in putting it there. As time wore on, it was Rangers, not Aberdeen, who began to look the more likely side to take the Cup and every Aberdeen fan in the ground was indebted to Jim Leighton for a truly magnificent save from Jim Bett in the last minute of normal time.

So began the extra thirty minutes, Aberdeen curiously leaden-footed and not looking particularly likely to score. The support was quiet and subdued, matching the mood of their side. Even the perky little Gordon Strachan, usually the most ebullient of players, did not seem particularly to want the ball. Nothing seemed more certain than that there would have to be a replay, and then, as so often happens, a goal came at the most improbable moment. It was a scrappy goal, appropriate that it should win a scrappy match. It came with only four minutes to go and it was hard that it should start with a mistake by Bobby Russell who had been quite outstanding. His crossfield pass was intercepted by Simpson who immediately found Eric Black. He in turn found Mark McGhee but it is doubtful whether he could have made the penalty area in time for the cross, had it not taken a deflection. McGhee's cross struck Craig Paterson, spun high and slow into the air and was hovering nicely when Black eventually came up to stoop and send a simple header beyond the hurtling, straining figure of Peter McCloy. It was a winner and also Aberdeen's 600th Scottish Cup goal.

Rangers were shattered, as well they might have been, and in the few minutes remaining, never looked like getting back on an equal footing. They knew that they had done at least enough to deserve a replay and they had been denied this by an unkind break of the ball. John Greig was able to assure his players that they had done well and he made the point forcibly that he considered that his side had not been well served by fortune:

"Other clubs set out to stop Gordon Strachan, but I put a footballer on him, Bobby Russell, and Bobby Russell came out a mile on top. We were the better side all the way through and I thought that we were unlucky losers."

Down the corridor, in the winners' dressing-room, things were very different and a white-faced Alex Ferguson emerged some minutes later to give an extraordinary press conference in which he lambasted his own players with a fierce vehemence:

"Two players won that Cup for us today. Alex and Willie, they played Rangers by themselves. McLeish in particular was out of this world considering that he was doubtful until the last minute. That was our only bright spot. The team looked tired, dead. There was no spark or movement about them. It was all square passing stuff-nothing football. We were lucky to win." He went on to elaborate on his thoughts.

"If Aberdeen players think that I am going to accept that standard then I'll be looking for new players next season. The only excuse I can make is that they looked knackered, as if they all needed a holiday. I'm still not prepared to accept it."

It was an astonishing outburst from the manager of a side which had just won two major competitions and narrowly failed to take a third. Mature reflection however showed the manager that while his assessment had been strictly accurate if one took the Scottish Cup Final in isolation, it was unwise so to do, and he had to remember that he was in charge of human beings, rather than automatons. It was greatly to Alex Ferguson's credit that he came to realise that his reaction had been intemperate and precipitate, and his apology was as public as his initial condemnation had been.

"I made a public apology to the players at St Andrews last night. (The Aberdeen side had held their celebration dinner there on the way back north.) I told them that my comments were made at a vulnerable time. I myself am tired and need a holiday, I haven't slept properly since coming home from Gothenburg. On Saturday, I felt deep frustration at the course the match was taking and sitting there in the dug-out I was unable to do very much about it. I spoke out to the media afterwards before I had had time to compose myself.

"Sheer courage won us the trophy. On reflection, I could see that the team had hit its peak in Sweden and that should properly have been the finale to the season. It was asking too much of themselves to lift themselves again so soon. These are players at the peak of their careers and we have set a standard which I think we are capable of repeating."

The manager's judgement proved to be correct and his prompt and honest offer of amends prevented a damaging gulf from appearing between himself and his senior players. There would be no better testimony that there had been no lasting damage caused than the fact that Aberdeen were to win the League Championship in each of the two following years. In the middle 1980s, it could be argued with a great deal of plausibility that the balance of power in Scottish football had, for the time being at least, shifted to the North-East.

One of that day's opponents, Jim Bett, would eventually land up at Pittodrie, having first honed his footballing skills in a European environment with the Belgian club, Lokeren. That was for the future. More immediate was the chance that would be presented the following year for Aberdeen to join Rangers and Queen's Park in taking the Scottish Cup for a third consecutive year. And the players were learning about the little attentions that are paid to players of a side as good as Aberdeen had become. On arriving at the Old Course Hotel at St Andrews, they found that the door handles had been painted red and white. Reception was draped in red and white and the traditional tall hat of the chef had been covered with a red stocking. To keep the theme consistent, the sweet chosen for the evening meal was raspberries and cream. It would have been a blasé player indeed who did not feel that he had arrived!

1983 ABERDEEN v. RANGERS. Eric Black made a habit of scoring important goals in Scottish Cup ties and none was more crucial than this header which gave Dons the Scottish Cup in 1983.

1983 — WILLIE MILLER REMEMBERS

We suffered in 1983 as a result of winning the Cup Winners Cup against Real Madrid at Gothenburg. It was a great performance, sure, but funnily enough I don't think we quite realised at the time just what we had done. Overnight we became well-known and this showed in a lot of ways, for example the club and the players began to get quite a lot of letters from abroad.

We had begun to think we would win the Cup Winners Cup after we beat Bayern in the quarter-finals. We always rated West German teams highly because we had been drawn against them often before, Fortuna Dusseldorf, Eintracht Frankfurt, S.V. Hamburg. These teams had done us a lot of damage in European competition so when we put out Bayern we began to think that we could maybe go all the way.

We honestly were a much better team than Rangers at the time of the final but we did not play at all well and after ninety minutes, had nothing to show for it. This did not worry us too much. We knew it was a mental tiredness rather than a physical one and that we were pretty fit really. We felt that if we could keep Rangers out there long enough we would wear them down although if Jim Leighton hadn't made another marvellous save just before the end of normal time, we would have been out. I couldn't have seen us finding anything in our jaded mood and in any case there would hardly have been time.

The goal itself was a bit scrappy but we grabbed it thankfully for it had always from the beginning of the second-half looked like a one-goal game. Eric Black switched the ball out right to Mark McGhee and could hardly have been up for the return cross but it spun off a defender's foot and slowed up in the air. In the end, he seemed to arrive at the ball quite slowly and deliberately and head it calmly into the net.

There was fun and games after the match of course with Fergie tearing into the team for not having played particularly well, not at all well in his estimation. As it happened, it was quite awkward for me for he singled out big Alex McLeish and myself as being the only two players worth a damn that day. I can tell you we took some ribbing from the rest of the boys along the lines of "teacher's pet". The others were pretty mad at the time for it really had been a very difficult thing to raise ourselves for another supreme effort so soon, and in the eyes of the world that European match was much the more important. But Fergie soon mended fences by apologising — he was good that way — and he had a young side that would have run through a wall for him.

When he came at first he was unhappy with the attitude he found in the dressing room and felt that five or six of the senior players were intriguing against him and were not open to persuasion. You never got blasé about Cup finals, no matter how many you played in, but sometimes at the end you could not react because you were drained of emotion. I remember getting a letter from the leader of a religious group who said that he'd been disgusted to see that as I lifted the Scottish Cup, my face was quite expressionless. He said that it was obvious to him that I'd won so many medals that I was bored by it all. It wasn't that at all, merely that you are very exhausted, physically and mentally, at the end of a hard-fought match.

1983 ABERDEEN v. RANGERS. Alex. McLeish is "crowned" by Mark McGhee after the second win over Rangers in consecutive years.

CHAPTER ELEVEN

1984 v. CELTIC

UPSIDES WITH RANGERS AND QUEEN'S PARK

The Scottish Cup Final of 1984 gave Aberdeen the opportunity to record a third consecutive win in the competition, something that only Rangers had accomplished in modern times. True, Queen's Park had twice won the Cup three times in a row, but that was in the earliest days of Association Football in Scotland and well before the emergence of some of the strongest clubs.

Ferguson had got Aberdeen brimming with confidence, city and club, to the extent that some of the Dons supporters now automatically pencilled in the Cup Final date for a jaunt to Glasgow. Yet this was a year when in the run-up to Hampden, the Reds lived extremely dangerously. In their very first cup-tie, they seemed to have been awarded an easy passage with a home draw against Kilmarnock but they struggled to an uneasy 1-1 draw and were glad enough to get a second chance back at Rugby Park. They took it convincingly enough with a 3-1 win and were rather more on their guard for a similar visit to Shawfield where they won 2-0 at the first time of asking. In the quarter-final, Dundee United managed a goalless draw at Pittodrie, that was no great surprise since the Tannadice club had a very good record there and perhaps home advantage counted for less in matches between these two than on more other occasions. It would certainly appear to be so for Aberdeen scraped through by a single goal in the replay and won their first semi-final with a bit in hand, the senior Dundee club going down 2-0.

Nine of the Aberdeen side had been there the previous season when Rangers had been beaten for the second time. For once in a way, in meetings between Aberdeen and Celtic, it would be the northern side which would be going into the match far more experienced in Scottish Cup Final situations. Alex Ferguson, with a seven point margin in the championship over second-placed Celtic — an identical difference would separate the clubs the following year — was not the man to pass up lightly the considerable psychological advantage which this situation conferred on Aberdeen:

"No one can say that Celtic are not an ambitious club but for all their ambition they were not good enough to win the championship."

Second place had not been a bad performance for them, however, and the team they fielded on the day of the Final would take a deal of beating. In goal, the big Irishman, Pat Bonner, had already given evidence that he was one of the best goalkeepers in the country and in years to come would extend that to being one of the best in Europe. Danny McGrain was approaching the end of the road but was unexcelled in making the head save the legs, besides which he had considerable inspirational qualities. Mark Reid, the other back, was a younger player but had known the big occasion before and had scored from a penalty at Hampden to save a League Cup final with only one minute left. No one need question his nerve.

The great galvaniser of the Celtic side was Roy Aitken, a Celtic player since the age of 17 and a better footballer than his detractors were prepared to allow. While he was in charge, a team-mate would let his head droop to his peril. In the middle was Willie McStay who had spent much of his time at Parkhead in the shadows of the reserve team but would now emerge on this gala day to line up alongside his brother, Paul. The sturdy Murdo MacLeod would bustle about like a tug in mid-field and was a very useful man if a free kick came Celtic's way anywhere within 40 yards of goal.

Davie Provan was at a peak from which he was abruptly to be struck down by M.E.; no one going to the game could know this, but his career was effectively almost at an end. Paul McStay was the personification of artistry, incapable of an ungraceful movement, although there were some who said that his development had slowed since the prodigy that was Charlie Nicholas had left Parkhead for a more sedate career with Arsenal. Frank McGarvie could upset the most composed defences with his unselfish running, and persistent worrying created chances for more orthodox colleagues. Tommy Burns was the thinker of the side, not always able to keep himself above the hurly-burly but with all the talents needed to make a first-class player. The team was completed by the signing of the Motherwell player, Brian McClair who, as Manchester United would later prove, gave you two players for the price of one, since he could be equally effective as a striker or in mid-field. This added up to a team which would not easily yield the day and if spur were needed, there was the matter of that lost League championship. It was always possible that Fergie's words uttered at an Open Day for the media, might return to plague him.

There had been a macabre and tragic start to the day for those who came down from the north when a supporter, who had apparently been persuaded to make the trip on the roof of a train, was swept off and fell to his death near Arbroath. There was a very numerous contingent of Aberdeen supporters anxious to be present at an occasion which might well see footballing history made. These were the teams who would be given the chance to do it:

ABERDEEN: Leighton; McKimmie, Rougvie, Cooper, McLeish, Miller, Strachan, Simpson, McGhee, Black, Weir. Substitutes: Stark, Bell.

CELTIC: Bonner; McGrain, Reid, Aitken, W McStay, MacLeod, Provan, P McStay, McGarvey, Burns, McClair. Substitutes: Melrose, Sinclair.

Right from the start, there was a frenetic atmosphere to the match. Aberdeen-Celtic fixtures had in recent years acquired an excessively combative tinge, the Dons seeing themselves as the New Establishment, Celtic resistant and resentful at any attempt to topple them from their position of preeminence. Matters were not helped by the first Aberdeen goal which arrived in the early stages. Following a Strachan corner on the right, McLeish headed the ball on and Eric Black, who must have been very close to being offside, squeezed the ball up and over the lunging Pat Bonner. Referee Bob Valentine looked enquiringly at his enclosure-side linesman, Eric Black did the same a touch guiltily, but the flag stayed down and Aberdeen were ahead. As the ball was being re-centred, an exchange of views between Strachan and Aitken boded ill for the rest of the match.

Celtic fought back, time was still on their side and Jim Leighton was alert and able in the Aberdeen goal. Even then he was obliged to Stewart McKimmie, who had never even played at Hampden but who now booted a shot off the line when Murdo MacLeod thought that he had equalised. This was in 35 minutes and two minutes later Hampden Park was like Bedlam.

The Celtic captain, Roy Aitken, brought down Mark McGhee — they would live to be team-mates — with a tackle which was certainly a heavy one. The Aberdeen player needed some considerable treatment and while this was being administered, Strachan and Aitken were seen once again chipping away at each other. Satisfied that McGhee had recovered, referee Bob Valentine then approached Roy Aitken who stood penitent and prepared to receive a yellow card.

The card was red in colour and Aitken stood disbelieving. For a moment, it looked as if he might not go, then he shook his head angrily and departed for the pavilion, not before a final exchange with Strachan. He had become the first player to be ordered from the field in a Scottish Cup final since Jock Buchanan of Rangers in 1929, and indeed they were the only two players in the entire history of the competition who had incurred the maximum penalty.

The decision to send off caused a great deal of argument. Aitken was known to be a vigorous and occasionally clumsy player but he had never been regarded as malevolent. Having said that, some of the argument brought forward against his dismissal was illogical, none more so than the complaint that this sort of thing, a sending-off, should not happen in a Scottish Cup final. What the adherents of this point of view were arguing, even if they did not realise it, was that a Cup final should not be refereed according to the normal laws of the game. If Bob Valentine was convinced that he would have

1984 ABERDEEN v. CELTIC. OH NO, NOT THE RED CARD! Roy Aitken of Celtic looks angry and aghast as the realisation dawns that he has been ordered from the field after only half an hour of the Scottish Cup Final of 1984. Referee Bob Valentine is the man in charge who too the decision.

ordered Roy Aitken off in less exalted circumstances, then his
decision had to be the same.

The distraught Aitken vanished up the tunnel and
Celtic were left to contemplate playing for almost an hour with
only ten men. Out on the field, the atmosphere continued to be
bad with frequent bookings, six names in all would go into the
book. Strachan, himself cautioned for a prior foul on Aitken,
came in for some heavy treatment from Celtic players who
clearly felt that he had attempted to persuade the referee to send
Aitken off. The game metaphorically limped towards half time
and several players limped literally.

At half time, Alex Ferguson was worried and made the
point that Aberdeen were now facing a bigger problem in
confronting ten men. He may have made too much of this and
over-influenced his own players, because for the rest of the
normal ninety minutes, Aberdeen fell more and more out of the
game. The Celtic response was heroic. McClair ran himself
into the earth in mid-field, so too MacLeod. Willie McStay,
only in the side because of an injury to Tom McAdam, could not
have acquitted himself better.

Aberdeen grew more and more jittery as the warm
afternoon passed. Celtic, picking up in confidence, began to
press forward. It was as if the weight of the attempt at the treble
had got to the Aberdeen players and they rarely looked like
increasing their lead, even with an advantage in numbers.
Several times the Aberdeen goal was put under severe threat but
survived, and it began to look as if that early, contested goal
from Eric Black would do it.

With five minutes to go, Alex Ferguson's dread was
realised when Celtic scored the equaliser, a quite magnificent
goal. The build-up was from Danny McGrain and Jim Melrose
who had come on as substitute for Mark Reid in a typical piece
of positive thinking in a ten man situation. The ball was slipped
to Paul McStay who had a fierce shot which he employed much
too seldom for the liking of his many admirers. This afternoon
he proved their point by smashing a rising drive far beyond the
stretching Jim Leighton.

Celtic were back on terms but here the revised arrangements for the Scottish Cup Final worked against them. Until
three years before, their task would merely have been to hang
on for another few minutes and then try all over again in the

replay, with spirits high because of a successful rearguard action with a depleted side. Since 1981 and two dreadful goalless matches between Rangers and Hibernian which necessitated a third meeting of the clubs, it had been decided that there would be extra time played on the occasion of the first game. Aberdeen were now going to achieve another, unwanted treble, extra time in three consecutive Scottish Cup finals, and Celtic's task was therefore to survive not for another five minutes, but for thirty five.

In the end, it proved just beyond them, although again the winning goal required the involvement of a substitute, this time Dougie Bell, who had come on to the field to replace Peter Weir. It was a fine goal, though in the end a rather strange one. It looked like a story-book ending for those in the stand sitting behind the line of Bell's thirty yarder which soared to the right-hand postage stamp corner of Bonner's goal. It eluded the keeper's straining finger-tips by about a foot, only to crash into play again off the angle of crossbar and goalpost. The force of the shot took the rebound far out to the right wing. Immediately, the busy Strachan returned it across goal and with the Celtic defence still thinking in terms of reprieve and survival, McGhee did very well to force the ball home from a tight angle.

Celtic this time could not find a response, the legs had gone though the hearts kept pumping. Aberdeen had made it three in a row, winning 18 Scottish Cup ties in the process, and had become the first club outside Glasgow ever to claim that distinction. Celtic, the team with the greatest Cup record of all, had never managed to do it, even in the headiest days of Jock Stein.

More parades, more speeches, unbridled enthusiasm on the part of the supporters back home. The summer of 1984 saw the coal strike at its height and there was a special point to the banner displayed for the benefit of the returning team: "Willie Miller stops more strikers than the police". A second banner, equally witty, bore the legend: "Another poor harvest for Hay and McGrain". Aberdeen were at last a power in the land, quite entitled to consider themselves the equal of Celtic and Rangers and perhaps at that moment, their superior.

The question was for how long could this happy state of affairs last, for there were considerable movements brewing at the club. That cross from Strachan and its astute conversion by

McGhee would be the last contributions that either would make in an Aberdeen jersey. Following the accepted if rather peculiar modern pattern, they were moving on at the height of their success and leaving a club which had few superiors in Europe at that moment.

Gordon Strachan would go to Old Trafford. He could be an irritating little man to play against, chirping throughout the entire game, but he had an almost-lost ability and belief to beat an opponent, the essential touch of cockiness which the good player must have in the fiercely competitive world of the professional footballer. He was not a Glasgow man but the Glasgow adjective "gallus" sat well upon him. He would prove over several seasons to be a very good buy for Manchester United and with profit might have been given a more responsible role for his country.

Mark McGhee went off to Europe where his reflective intelligence served him well with Hamburg. He also acquired the toughness to realise that big signings are not automatically welcomed by everyone on the staff of the club to which they have gone, especially by those whose own positions are now under threat. He would return to Scotland and win a medal with Celtic and in the dying days of his career, was reunited with Roy Aitken as a Newcastle United player.

Doug Rougvie, target of opposition fans, gap-toothed, cheerful, soaked in blood or sweat and sometimes both, was also about to make his farewells to Pittodrie. He was signing for Chelsea and there did seem something incongruous about the association of the buirdly Doug with that rather effete district of London. A large bite had been taken out of the Cup Final side, but in public at any rate the manager remained optimistic.

"We know that Strachan and McGhee want away. We are sorry to see them go but the Dons will not crumble just because a couple of men are leaving. The one thing in football is that it keeps throwing up new players and it could be that the vacancies occurring now are just what is needed to create opportunities for youngsters on the staff, players like Ian Porteous who has perhaps suffered from being too like Gordon Strachan."

From most men, even from most football managers - a special breed of men - that might well have been dismissed as putting a good face on things, mere whistling in the wind.

Ferguson however meant what he said. He knew that just before the Cup Final, Aberdeen had played a League match at Paisley and gone down narrowly 3-2. What was important about that was the number of star players missing from his side that night. Strachan, McLeish, Miller, Simpson, Bell, Weir and Black were all absent at Love Street and yet another Premier Division club had been given a hard-enough game in all conscience.

The three stars duly went. The world continued to spin and it was not the end of civilisation as we know it. On the contrary, Aberdeen retained their League championship the following year. In 1986, the year after that, they renewed their acquaintanceship with Hampden on Cup Final day. As a writer in the Press and Journal neatly put it: "If there are any more triumphs the open-top bus will have to be put on the regular city bus time-table".

1984 ABERDEEN v. CELTIC. Mark McGhee, out of picture, scores with almost his last kick as a competitive player for Aberdeen. Bonner, McGrain and MacLeod are unable to do anything about this winning goal in the 1984 Cup Final.

1984 — WILLIE MILLER REMEMBERS

When you play the Old Firm in Glasgow, you will always have the crowd to contend with, yet the two sides give you a different game. Rangers are strong physically, well-organised, while Celtic are more improvised, more inspirational and playing the ball cleverly to feet. I preferred the Rangers games because they were easier for a defender to plan. Challenge strongly, win the ball, deny possession. You could be sure that both sides would come at you in waves from the start but whereas Rangers might well protect a lead, Celtic would keep on attacking even if well ahead because prolonged defence was not something which suited them.

You said that you had some doubt about the first Aberdeen goal that day. Eric Black's. In defence you can never judge offside, 30-40 yards ahead, but I remember we felt that we had had some very adverse decisions in finals in Glasgow, decisions that had cost us Cup medals and we were therefore not apologetic about the goal or likely to look at it too closely. If you like, it was a rub of the green.

My immediate reaction to the Roy Aitken tackle was that it was a red card one although I'd be inclined to agree now that it looked worse than it actually was. Roy was not a malevolent or a vicious tackler, but he was clumsy, a good player but not an especially good tackler. It was a surprising challenge for such an experienced player to make but he was an enormous loss to Celtic because he undoubtedly drove the side.

We had a bad second-half but again I don't think it was because we consciously tried to defend a one-goal lead. Fergie had been quite kind to us at half-time and I had noticed before that just occasionally, when he had maybe over-praised us — and it was just occasionally, believe me — we sometimes took the foot off the accelerator and allowed the other side back into the game.

I can't say we were all that worried. After all in the two previous years we had beaten 11 men over 120 minutes so we could surely do the same for ten.

Dougie Bell's shot which came back off the bar was a beauty. The Celtic defence had given it up as a goal and just for a minute I think they were caught off guard. At any rate when it came out right we whipped it back across the goal and Mark

McGhee got the winner. We had won the Cup three times on the trot and only Rangers and Queen's Park I think had ever done that.

And yet it was a disappointing time too because Mark McGhee, Gordon Strachan and Doug Rougvie all opted to go off to play in England. I get angry when papers write that this is inevitable for a club like Aberdeen. I don't see why it should be in the least inevitable, this is a big club even by European standards and we have the example of Dundee United who have managed to hold on to the great bulk of their players with a much smaller support. Still, even with that, we had won the Scottish three times in a row even although we had worked overtime each time to do it.

CHAPTER TWELVE

1986 v. HEARTS

ABERDEEN ANGUS

There is a well-known Hollywood cliché in which the hero has been thrashed round a boxing ring by some unappealing hulk and is on the point of being counted out when he is saved by the gong. Swift treatment and magic words transform him in the space of a minute into a raging fury who goes forth to knock seven bells out of his opponent. In real boxing terms, the sound of the bell serves almost always only to postpone the inevitable and this was certainly the case with Heart of Midlothian in 1986.

It is doubtful if ever a side came into a Scottish Cup final in more depressing circumstances. The previous Saturday, they had gone to Dens Park, Dundee, for their last League match of the season and all they required to do was to avoid defeat for the League championship to be theirs for the first time since 1960. They had gone 31 games unbeaten and although Celtic, who required to beat St Mirren at Paisley by the proverbial barrowload, immediately put pressure on Hearts by doing just that — they were four up at half-time — that would avail Celtic nothing unless Hearts lost, and with a mere seven minutes to go, they were holding Dundee to a nervy but adequate goalless draw, although the Celtic players had errone-ously been told that Hearts were behind.

Enter one Albert Kidd, who had been pulled off the

Dundee bench with half an hour to go. He scored and the news, communicated by jungle drum and transistor to Love Street, set the terraces there aflame. Four minutes later, Kidd scored again. The author remembers this second goal very vividly because he was at Ibrox covering Graeme Souness's first game in charge of Rangers, their opponents being Motherwell. In his excitement the commentator at Dens Park first said that Walter Kidd — the Hearts captain — had scored and wave upon wave of cheering rocked the stadium. It ceased as though a sponge had been taken across the seats of the Ibrox stands as the commentator hastily corrected Hearts' Walter to Dundee's Albert. Dundee had won 2-0 and Hearts had had the title snatched from them at the last possible moment, leaving their dual managership team of Alex MacDonald and Sandy Jardine with the Herculean task of restoring morale in the short space of a week.

Hearts could argue that they had been unlucky in that last game, although the major reason for their failure had simply been that in the crunch the nerve had gone. There had been a virus in the Tynecastle dressing-room which had deprived them of their promising young player, Craig Levein, and had meant four others on their playing staff had operated below their best capabilities. Alex MacDonald knew that this was not a moment for that most dangerous of footballing indulgences, self-pity.

"What happened at Dens Park is history. I know that we are in danger of getting more sympathy than Celtic are praise and that would be wrong. If we can win the Cup then it is hardly a wash-out season."

Aberdeen by comparison were apparently trouble-free. They had seldom gone to the final of a Scottish Cup with so little travelling to do. Severe winter weather had forced the postponement of their first-round tie against Montrose from January 25 to February 5, but when the game was played, rank asserted itself and in winning 4-1, Aberdeen were never extended. From then on, they did not have to go south of Angus for they made three visits to that county. Tight and windy Gayfield always provided the possibility of an upset and the Dons were grateful to Joe Miller for his goal which took them through against Arbroath.

In the next round, an away draw against Dundee was

likewise potentially perilous and Aberdeen needed a home replay to get the better of the Dark Blues, John Hewitt being much in evidence. For once in the semi-final, Aberdeen supporters did not have to make the long trip to Glasgow, the S.F.A. sensibly deciding that Dens Park would make a good venue for the semi-final tie with Hibernian. This proved to be almost the easiest of all Aberdeen's matches, Billy Stark, Eric Black and Joe Miller scoring in an emphatic Dons victory.

On that dramatic day when Hearts and Celtic disputed the League flag, Aberdeen were playing before a handful of spectators at Clydebank, but they were in even more prolific scoring form than Celtic that day. By half time, they led 5-0 and the goals had gone to Stark, McMaster, Weir, Hewitt and McDougall, a multi-barrel form of attack which could only please any manager. It was incidentally a savage farewell to Jim Fallon, the long-serving Clydebank defender.

Aberdeen would therefore come to the Cup Final as the hottest of favourites, although there was always the chance of a ferocious reaction from a thwarted Hearts side. Once again, it was a World Cup year and the relative standings of the sides can be seen in the fact that four Dons, Leighton, Miller, McLeish and Bett, would made the trip to Mexico, while Tynecastle would not have a single representative. Four was a considerable contribution although, to keep Aberdeen feet on the ground, Dundee United's Jim McLean could have pointed out that he would be sending five players.

When everything seems clear in Association football, it is a fair bet that what P G Wodehouse used to call the Divine Sandbag will be produced. So it proved this time when, with a few days to go, Alex Ferguson announced that Eric Black would not be considered for a place in the Hampden squad. He gave his reasons at some length.

"Eric Black will take no part in the Scottish Cup Final. He has played his last game for us. I feel it only fair to the other players who have been loyal to the club that he should take no part on Saturday.

"It was a painful and difficult decision to make but I feel it was the right one. The player's contract is not up until June 30, but he has signed for Metz. Aberdeen will have nothing to do with agents for any player. Someone has to take a stand against this practice and show their displeasure with what is

going on. We are big enough to do that by not playing Eric Black
against Hearts on Saturday.

"It is really a sad end to Eric Black's career at Aberdeen.
He has been with us since he was 13, through all our ups and
downs. When he had a severe back complaint we stuck by him.
It is a great pity that it has happened this way but his decision
to deal through an agent has cost him his place on Saturday. He
has now gone to an insignificant club in Europe and his agent
has done him no favours at all. It is a travesty that Eric Black,
a player like him, should be going to a club like Metz."

As ever, what is important is what is not said. Alex
Ferguson's displeasure was not based on the fact that Black had
moved, he recognised that a player had the right to better
himself and indeed he himself would be on the move within
months. He had however a deep-seated dislike for agents which
originated in the days of the Gordon Strachan transfer. Whatever the background, and he genuinely felt that Eric Black could
have done better for himself, a belief partly borne out by events,
it was a highly courageous decision to do without the player in
the Final. Black already had three Scottish Cup medals as a
young player and was without doubt a lad for the big occasion.
Only a few months before, he had scored twice in the League
Cup Final success against Hibernian at Hampden, and in his
entire Aberdeen career managed 79 goals in just 215 games.
Fergie however felt that the vital thing was to encourage the
others and Black did not play. To his credit, the player did not
react angrily and said all the right things in public about the
forthcoming match in a dignified manner.

The sides that took the field for the Cup Final were
these.

ABERDEEN: Leighton; McKimmie, McQueen,
McMaster, McLeish, W Miller, Hewitt, Cooper, McDougall,
Bett, Weir. Substitutes: Stark, J Miller.

HEARTS: Smith; Kidd, Whittaker, Jardine, Berry, Levein,
Colquhoun, Black, Clark, Mackay, Robertson.

In an Aberdeen side in which six players had played
more than 200 games, Tommy McQueen was a young player
bursting through and John McMaster was one who had made an
almost fictional come-back from an injury which had appeared
so serious that 18,000 supporters had attended his benefit game
earlier in the season. By January, he was displaying such

consistency that there was no excluding him. Up front, the strong, bustling Frank McDougall had reinforced the St Mirren connection which Peter Weir and Billy Stark had set, while the youthful Joe Miller was beginning to elbow aside his more senior forwards.

The Hearts achievement should not be minimised. A handful of years before, Wallace Mercer had taken charge of an ailing, moribund club and by his drive and enthusiasm, he had transformed it into what it always ought to be, a leading force in Scottish football. So far had Hearts slipped that when Mercer took over, the club was forbidden to deal in the registration of players. Mixing shrewdness with sheer hard work, Mercer effected a speedy transformation.

He opted for dual managership, Sandy Jardine on the field, Alex MacDonald off, and for about five seasons, this arrangement worked very well. In goal, Hearts had the dependable Henry Smith from Leeds United for whom Hampden would later prove to be not the most fortunate of grounds. Walter Kidd, all effort and earnest endeavour, was captain and right-back in the old phrase, and he could be guaranteed to lead by example. His partner, Brian Whittaker, was the more gifted footballer but at times could appear dangerously languid in defence. Alongside Jardine in midfield was the solid Neil Berry, an excellent acquisition from England, and Craig Levein who even then was being tipped as a Scotland player.

Up front, the speed and thrust of the articulate John Colquhoun was balanced by the strength of Kenny Black and Sandy Clark, the latter being an intriguing mixture of elbows and considerable ball skill, while Hearts demonstrated that they not only bought players but developed their own in the persons of the two remaining Maroons, Gary Mackay and John Robertson, the one a creator, the other a natural goal-scorer.

The old hand, Sandy Jardine, knew how important it was to lighten the situation if at all possible and he did this in an interview he gave before the game.

"It is my tenth Cup Final and I'll enjoy it every bit as much as my first. I'll enjoy it win, lose or draw. At my age it's a dream come true just to be taking part in the final. There can only be about four left for me!" His team-mate and skipper, Walter Kidd, offered a sadly unprophetic view of events. "I am

167

definitely going to enjoy it because I don't know if I'll ever get there again."

Despite the crushing events of the previous week, which had seen Hearts supporters, their heads muffled in scarves, weeping in the streets of Dundee, there was a majority of Edinburgh folk in the 62,841 crowd, it having been estimated that around 35,000 of those had come through from the Capital. Within a few minutes their world had fallen in about their ears and John Hewitt was the man responsible.

Hewitt had a reputation for being quick off the mark in more senses than one. He held the record for the quickest Scottish Cup goal ever recorded for it had taken him just 9.6 seconds to find the net against Motherwell in 1983. He was not quite so quick on this occasion, as a whole five minutes had passed before he struck. The goal did not show the Edinburgh defence in a good light. Hewitt collected a ball on the right, almost on the half-way line, Willie Miller the supplier, and set out for goal. As he closed in, there was surprisingly no challenge from Neil Berry or Brian Whittaker and Hewitt's left-foot shot was too accurately placed for Henry Smith. Aberdeen were ahead.

For the remainder of the match, Aberdeen only seemed under serious threat on one occasion. That was as early as the 18th minute when, after Berry headed down a cross from the right, Robertson found himself completely in the clear. It was the kind of chance that he put away at training with monotonous regularity, except of course that this was not a training session but a Scottish Cup final. The little forward snatched at it and his first-time lob cleared Jim Leighton but also the crossbar very comfortably. For the remaining 70 minutes, Alex McLeish, playing in a pair of boots hastily borrowed from reserve keeper Bryan Gunn — his own had been left behind at Pittodrie — was never troubled.

It was at least established that Hearts, behind as they were, now had to come forward. Inevitably, play got a little tousy and mixed, and before half time, Walter Kidd, the Hearts skipper, had been yellow-carded for a foul on Hewitt, and Neil Berry likewise for persistent dissent. There was just the one goal between the sides at half time and it was entirely possible that Alex MacDonald would find the right words to say to his team.

The man who rendered any such address useless was once again John Hewitt who clearly came back to the field after the break feeling that he had been over-dilatory in the first half for it took him precisely three minutes this time to put the game outwith the reach of Hearts. It was a textbook goal and owed much to the two former Saints. Peter Weir got away on the left and swept over a low probing cross. Frank McDougall stepped over the ball in a perfect dummy, taking a defender with him, and Hewitt was there to sweep the ball beyond Henry Smith. On the rejoicing Aberdeen bench, Alex Ferguson had a special cause for satisfaction when he reflected that John Hewitt had been his first-ever signing at Pittodrie.

And that was almost that. There remained two high-lights, one delightful, the other very sad. There was a third goal for Aberdeen and again it was a beauty. John McMaster had gone off to a hero's ovation and was replaced by the lanky Billy Stark. He it was who got the third goal and again the St Mirren influence was overwhelming. Peter Weir this time sent over a higher cross and Stark was most picturesquely parallel to the ground as he headed the ball home with great panache. There were fifteen minutes left and already up in the Directors' Box the red ribbon was being wreathed round the Scottish Cup.

As if to show that when Fate has got it in for you there are no half-measures, there was yet another disaster in store for the large but by now steadily dwindling Hearts support. Those who looked back over their shoulders as they climbed the steep Hampden terracing on the way out could see Walter Kidd in earnest conversation with referee Hugh Alexander. Walter Kidd had not had a happy afternoon. He had struggled against Peter Weir but bravely kept bursting forward and it was not only Hearts supporters who thought that he might well have earned a penalty when brought down by McQueen. Now at last the pent-up frustration of this Saturday and last had caught up with him. Already booked in the first half, he had been given the benefit of the doubt by Hugh Alexander on another occasion a few minutes before the third goal. But when he threw the ball in a fit of exasperation at two Aberdeen players, Weir and McDougall, there could be only one outcome. He became the third player, and the first captain, to be sent from the field in a Scottish Cup final and curiously Aberdeen had been involved in another of those sendings-off, that of Roy Aitken of Celtic in the club's previous visit to Hampden in 1984.

As Kidd mournfully trudged to the dressing-room, an abysmal end to what had started so proudly with his leading out the Hearts side less than two hours before, even the Aberdeen players felt sorry for their likeable and dejected opponent. The remaining few minutes of play were inevitably an anti-climax and everyone was glad when the final whistle sounded. The Hearts players slumped to the turf, a season which had promised them so much had ended by yielding them nothing tangible.

Commiseration is always a dangerous thing in football — for one thing it can be taken the wrong way by the defeated — and Alex Ferguson was cautious in his choice of words after the match.

"I was careful not to sympathise with Hearts after last week's result at Dundee because it could be taken as condescension on our part. In many ways, however, this season belongs to Hearts even if they finished without a trophy. They alone made a worthwhile League challenge and they brought the crowds back to Scottish football."

Sandy Jardine was left to take what consolation he could from the considerable honour of being named Player of the Year by the Scottish Football Writers. He must also have wondered privately if Hearts would ever be as close to a Scottish Cup medal again in whatever time he had left at the club. Incredibly, the Tynecastle side would be back in a semi-final against Celtic in the very near future and would blow a winning position in even more dramatic circumstances than on that fateful day at Dundee.

As for Aberdeen, success as ever meant change, but this time the most important change was off the field. Alex Ferguson decided in November 1986 that the time had come to move on and try his hand at managership in England. With him he took his recently-appointed assistant, Archie Knox.

Neither man had any practical first-hand experience of English football and the first few years in England were extremely taxing with stories of impending managerial change at Old Trafford, for they had gone to manage Manchester United

1986 TRIUMPH AND DESPAIR. As the game between Aberdeen and Hearts finishes Jim Leighton does his impression of a praying mantis while Henry Smith is the picture of depression.

171

and were the common currency of the tabloids. Ferguson and Knox held on however and in the early summer of 1990, their efforts were rewarded with the F.A. Cup, and Ferguson had in his managerial career successfully annexed the premier knock-out trophy in both Scotland and England.

The debt owed to him by Aberdeen in particular and Scottish football generally was enormous. Perhaps his major contribution during his reign at Pittodrie was that he instilled in his players not the hope but the expectation of winning, especially important in matches against the Old Firm. Ferguson managed to make his players believe that they were certainly as good, and in all probability better, than anything that Rangers or Celtic could field. He did this not as some other celebrated managers have done, in a kind of astounding confidence-trick, but because he genuinely believed this to be so. Moreover, his bounds were not set by the frontiers of Scotland. He saw Aberdeen as a genuine European force and Gothenburg in 1983 was abundantly to confirm that judgement.

Obsessively perfectionist, edgy, never willing to settle for second best, Alex Ferguson could be a hard manager, although he was never as unyielding as the legendary Eddie Turnbull. At times, the players could and did take him on and Steve Archibald did so on one very celebrated occasion involving a match ball. Ferguson had done a magnificent job for Aberdeen and the question of an adequate replacement would cause great concern. "Fergie" had brought not only outstanding ability and prodigious industry to the manager's office. He had just as importantly imparted continuity after the club's short spells in the charge of Alistair McLeod and Billy McNeill.

In the modern manner, Ferguson would take the player he liked best with him. That proved to be goalkeeper Jim Leighton who over ten years at Pittodrie had reached an unparalleled high level of consistency. He had been a model for any professional footballer to follow, but it is probable that his best days had been those at Pittodrie. When he moved to England, he found considerable difficulty in reproducing his highest form at either club or international level.

No matter how irreplaceable a manager, the attempt must be made immediately to replace him. Great surprise was caused by the eventual choice, Ian Porterfield. He had begun his career in Scotland as a player with Raith Rovers, but early on

1986 ABERDEEN v. HEARTS. Alex Ferguson consoles a heart-broken Sandy Jardine as the final whistle blows at Hampden. Hearts had lost the league through their defeat at Dundee the previous Saturday.

had moved south and was best known to football fans as the scorer of the goal which had given Sunderland the F.A. Cup against Leeds United in 1973. Subsequently, he had gone on to manage Sheffield United, another historical giant fallen upon evil days and in taking them from Division Four to Division Two of the Football League, might have been thought to have done well enough.

For this, he received the traditional reward of football managers - the sack - and although by any standards of fairness he had done well in England, his appointment to Pittodrie nevertheless took most watchers of Scottish football by surprise. The odd thing about the musical chairs scenario was that Manchester United were getting a managerial team who were new to the English situation while Porterfield was equally out of touch with developments in Scotland. In the end, he would fail but fail narrowly, and in the process contribute to two of the greatest club matches ever seen in Scotland, the Skol League Cup finals of 1988 and 1989 between Aberdeen and Rangers. Before the Dons would participate in another Scottish Cup final, however, there would require to be still one more change of manager at Pittodrie.

1986 — WILLIE MILLER REMEMBERS

This was the final we won in a canter. Hearts were still shell-shocked from the previous week at Dundee where they had lost the League championship in the last seven minutes of the match. Alex Ferguson warned us that our greatest danger would be in feeling sorry for them and while we were, I must say we did a most efficient job on them.

I suppose they were in the position that we had been in at Hampden in 1978, unused to the big occasion and a bit apprehensive about it. This time the opening burst would come from us and we made it pay with a John Hewitt goal early on and when we added a second after half-time, the game was over to all intents and purposes. One of our goals was a great diving header by Billy Stark, one of the squad men that Fergie used so well. He was marvellous at ghosting in at the far post, very good in the air and would get you 12-15 goals a season, a high strike rate for a midfield man.

We had several players like that. Dougie Bell, who never stopped running at defences, was used by Fergie almost as a European secret weapon. The Continentals had never seen a player like him and had no idea of how to cope with him. John McMaster was another, a brilliant left-foot and the ability to pass the defence-splitting long ball. He was badly hampered by the serious injury he picked up against Liverpool. He came back but his mobility was severely hampered and he was the kind of player who had always had to work hard at his mobility even when fully fit.

Through these years we managed to replace one good player with another. I think that especially applies to goalkeepers. I started with Bobby Clark and I suppose that his very best years were perhaps before I arrived at Pittodrie in 1971. He remained a very fine keeper however and a great influence on younger players in the dressing-roon. Jim Leighton was a fine keeper, brave and with an astonishing ability to make the crucial save when he had done virtually nothing in the rest of the game, like the famous save from Jim Bett of Rangers in the final of 1983. Jim's great weakness was kicking a dead ball. He dipped his left leg as he made contact and the dressing-room joke was that all over Aberdeen there were dozens of would-be

175

boy keepers who had skinned knees from trailing them along the ground in imitation of Jim.

When he went to Manchester United, we thought we must struggle but Theo Snelders has been the complete goalkeeper. The Dutch boys are very professional in their approach and the outfield players have lovely touches and great awareness.

The going of Fergie was a hammer blow. It meant I'd be on my sixth manager for I'd been signed when Eddie Turnbull was there and then spent three years or so under Jimmy Bonthrone, a lovely man and very well-liked by the players but who found it difficult to step up from trainer to manager. I believe that Alex Ferguson felt that he had done all that he could here, he'd won the three major domestic trophies and a European, but even then he might have stayed had it been any other club but Manchester United. It took him some time to adjust to England since neither he or Archie Knox had any first-hand experience of it but as we know he won the F.A. Cup last year.

The same was true in reverse for his successor at Aberdeen, Ian Porterfield, who had played almost all his football and done all his managing in England. It was rumoured at the time that Tommy Craig might be coming as his assistant and perhaps that would have worked better. Then the present manager, Alex Smith, came and of course we won two trophies last season.

CHAPTER THIRTEEN

1990 v. CELTIC

THE PENALTY OF FAILURE

Aberdeen had by 1990 established such a recent record in Scottish Cup finals that they tended to be the favourites whenever they got that length. Billy McNeill's percipient remark in 1978 had come true - by getting to a lot of finals you get to win a lot of finals.

If that were true, and it was, then Billy McNeill himself stood to be victim of the notion for his own Celtic side would provide the opposition in this, the latest of the 13 Scottish Cup finals that Aberdeen had reached. Celtic by their own demanding standards had experienced a terrible season. Ousted from the League Cup and never remotely challenging in the League, they had failed almost totally to provide the dashing, attacking play with which they were traditionally associated. And unfortunately, on the one night when they did and their new Polish signing Dziekanowski scored four brilliant goals in a European Cup tie against Partizan Belgrade, a porous defence at the other end threw goals away as quickly as the inspired Continental could score them, and Celtic went out.

Aberdeen by this time were under new management. Ian Porterfield had never quite given the impression of permanence, had never quite installed himself in the hearts of the

Aberdeen support. When he eventually went, the choice as replacement fell on a man who, like Alex Ferguson, had parted company with St Mirren after achieving what was for the Paisley club considerable success, the winning of the Scottish Cup against Dundee United in 1987. There the resemblance ended.

Alex Smith was authoritative but quiet, highly unlikely it might be thought ever to be banished from the dug-out for excessive shouting or attempted influencing of referees. He had served a long managerial apprenticeship with Stirling Albion, too long some thought, although good judges had taken note of the consistent stream of talented players that always seemed to follow each other into Annfield. His Paisley experience could have sickened him but he was offered a post on the Aberdeen coaching staff and eventually, the opportunity to become Ian Porterfield's successor. Almost immediately, he had success in what seemed likely at best to be a transitional season when at the third time of asking, the Dons beat Rangers in a League Cup final. Three times in a row the sides had met, each time the games had been outstanding. On the two previous occasions, Rangers had eventually won deservedly, now it was the turn of Aberdeen and their win was every bit as merited in that they had to survive the loss of a goal to a penalty award that could fairly be described as ludicrous.

It was clear that Smith, assisted by Jocky Scott and Drew Jarvie, had got Aberdeen believing in themselves once again and although Rangers never seriously looked under threat in the Premier Division — they made a grim start to the campaign but so too did Aberdeen — any challenge that they met came from Pittodrie.

For Celtic, it had been their worst season since the last year of Jock Stein's managership in 1978. One of the few highlights had been a single goal victory over a much more accomplished side when Aberdeen went to Parkhead just before New Year. Celtic probably deserved to win and on their lacklustre, uncommitted display that day, Aberdeen certainly deserved to lose. Since then the team had picked up and had been particularly free-scoring on their way to the final. Partick Thistle in the third round had briefly taken the lead at Firhill but were eventually torn apart with the big Dutchman, Willem Van der Ark, scoring a hat-trick. Enormously tall, he was a difficult man to play against, being capable of fine ball control and extreme awkwardness almost in the same movement.

Morton gave Aberdeen the only close match they met with up to the final, and Aberdeen had to work hard to negotiate successfully the loss of an early goal at Pittodrie. Even then, there was only 2-1 in it at the end. At the quarter-final stage, Hearts were expected to provide stern opposition but did not, the 4-1 win on home soil was as easy as it reads for the Dons. There was a similar score-line in the semi-final against Dundee United at Tynecastle where there was a statistical rarity to delight those who take account of such things. There may well have been two own goals scored in a Scottish Cup semi-final before then but it seems reasonable to claim uniqueness for two own goals by foreigners, in this case the Finn, Mixu Paate-lainen, and the Dutchman, Freddie Van der Hoorn.

By comparison Celtic had had an easy passage to the final. Given a bad fright by Forfar Athletic in their first outing at Station Park, they had then redeemed a catastrophic season by beating Rangers 1-0 at Parkhead, Tommy Coyne scraping a cross over the line from close-in. A draw against Dunfermline Athletic at East End Park was a good result and the job was done without fuss at the second time of asking. With the easy semi-final draw against Clydebank, Celtic profited as expected, although the First Division side resisted stoutly.

Nevertheless, Celtic were a poor side currently, even Celtic supporters were not slow to admit that and the club chairman, Jack McGinn, had categorically to deny rumours that Celtic were actively contemplating a change in manager-ship. In the usual sparring and skirmishing that precedes Cup finals, Aberdeen struck an important psychological blow when in the last meeting in the League between the clubs, days only before the Hampden match, they won 3-1 at Parkhead.

It was not so much the win that was remarkable as the composition of the Aberdeen side. Celtic were going for a place in Europe and the feelings of the other competing clubs can best be imagined when the red shirts took the field at Parkhead minus McLeish, Gillhaus, Nicholas, Mason, Bett, Connor and Grant. It looked as if Aberdeen had simply flung the points at Celtic, an impression which was considerably strengthened when the home side went ahead through Andy Walker after a mere four minutes.

From that moment on, the Dons took Celtic apart, none more so than young Eoin Jess playing wide on the right. He scored twice and another youngster, Watson, had the third. Celtic were in a bad way and it seemed that they had never recovered from the staggering pre-season blow of seeing their former striker, Maurice Johnstone, almost signed and sealed to return to Parkhead, suddenly opt to go elsewhere and that elsewhere was Ibrox Park. It would have been a dreadful buffet even had Johnstone done nothing for Rangers, and in fact almost from the start, he played very well.

In addition, Celtic stalwarts such as Tommy Burns and Roy Aitken had gone and in the case of the latter, this seemed almost unthinkable. It was difficult to avoid the impression that here was a club a little at odds with itself and ill-prepared for a forthcoming Scottish Cup final. It did not have much to offer except 100 years of an unsurpassed Scottish Cup record and the vital question was: Would that be enough?

It very nearly was. The great majority of those spectators who went along to Hampden Park expected a comfortable Aberdeen victory, the Aberdonians exultantly, the Celtic support sullenly and fearfully. They saw the following teams take the field:

ABERDEEN: Snelders; McKimmie, Robertson, Grant, McLeish, Irvine, Nicholas, Bett, Mason, Connor, Gillhaus. Substitutes: Watson, Jess.

CELTIC: Bonner; Wdowczyk, Rogan, Grant, Elliott, Whyte, Stark, McStay, Dziekanowski, Walker, Miller. Substitutes: Coyne, Galloway.

In the Aberdeen side, there were interesting inclusions and omissions. Theo Snelders had made Aberdeen fans forget totally that Jim Leighton had gone, no inconsiderable feat given the high standard of performance that Leighton had consistently maintained over his decade at Pittodrie. David Robertson at number three was astonishingly composed and comfortable coming forward for such a tall man. Brian Grant and Brian Irvine were two of the young players who had broken through. If any testament to Irvine's ability were needed, he was keeping the great Willie Miller out of the team. Up front, Mason was quick and direct, while Connor's prodigious industry tended to make people overlook the very real skill the player possessed. Jim Bett had the passing ability to unlock any defence and to release the two remaining Dons, Charlie Nicholas and Hans Gillhaus, the recently arrived third Dutchman. (The other, Willem Van der Ark, would have been most welcome after his Firhill hat-trick but a groin strain ruled him out of consideration.)

Gillhaus was a classy player and his coming had seemed to revive the blunted appetite of Charlie Nicholas. The latter was outstandingly gifted although motivation could sometimes be a problem. If your idea of a good player was one who spent his time tearing up and down the pitch retrieving desperate situations in his own defence, then Charlie was not your man. It had to be accepted that he would drift out of games for long periods and then make one or two passes which no one else on the field was capable of making. He was also notably unselfish for a striker and one of his great attributes was the ability to make other people play.

As against that, Celtic had a fine goalkeeper in Pat Bonner and indeed within a few short weeks, he would prove in Italy at the World Cup that he was one of the best in the world, let alone Scotland. At full-back, Celtic seemed vulnerable. Their other Pole, Darius Wdowczyk, was a fast and resourceful player coming forward, but seemed at times to be less securely grounded in defence. Anton Rogan too liked to come up front and was good at so doing, but was prone to alarming lapses of concentration in defensive situations.

Peter Grant's strength was in winning the ball rather than using it, Paul Elliott was a fine player and had the almost-total command in the air that his present manager had brought to the job. Many supporters thought that he was the best of the recent Parkhead signings. Derek Whyte was a cool and resourceful young defender and a fine specimen of that dying breed, the young player developed from within the club. The only other such was Paul McStay, full of thoughtful grace, whose admirers would have wished him only a little more of the cockiness with which Gordon Strachan had infuriated them. There were two ex-Dons in the side, Billy Stark, now at the end of his career but still with a great positional eye, and the scuttling, strong Joe Miller. Darius Dziekanowski, inevitably Jackie to the Celtic support, had hit Parkhead on arrival with the force of a hurricane but his first burst of heavy scoring had tailed off about November. Since then, he had done little that was remarkable and in his own slump, he seemed to have affected the form of the remaining Celt, ex-Motherwell player Andy Walker.

As often happens, what was to be a wretched game gave promise of something better in the first few minutes. Almost from kick-off, Dziekanowski broke through the Aberdeen outer defence but his stumble in the penalty area was far too contrived to carry any conviction for referee George Smith, and the tall Pole's claims for a penalty were brusquely waved aside.

In the eighth minute came perhaps the highlight of the game. A Bett cross was feebly pushed away by Pat Bonner — the big keeper was uncharacteristically shaky throughout the first half — and the ball fell to Charlie Nicholas who had his back to goal. He pivoted swiftly and his quick turn deceived the Celtic defence. He sent the ball swiftly towards the empty net with Bonner stranded, but Paul Elliott had got back and, marvellously resisting the temptation to stick out a hand and concede the penalty, he stretched out a long leg instead and diverted the ball to safety. In retrospect, it would almost certainly have made for a better match had the ball gone in then.

Bonner, still apparently nervous, required two grabs at a not too taxing shot from Jim Bett and with one exception, that concluded the highlights of a sterile first half. The exception came just before the interval when Rogan broke down the left wing and pitched over a fine probing cross which the flying Stark headed inches over the crossbar. He had come very near to scoring against Aberdeen exactly the kind of goal he had scored for them against Hearts four years before.

Opinion on the terracings over half time was that the second half was bound to be better than the first, but in truth, very little improvement was apparent to the eye. Charlie Nicholas broke free of the anonymity that had shrouded him for much of the game and picked out Gillhaus with a pin-pointed cross but his Dutch colleague was a shade too deliberate with his header and found the side netting rather than the back of it. At the other end, Stark with another header which went narrowly past demonstrated that he would be left unattended at Aberdeen's peril.

In 65 minutes, Elliott collected a yellow card which brought his total for the season to thirteen, though this one, as one or two others, seemed scarcely merited. If Elliott was unlucky — and it seemed a case of the player's reputation rather than the actual foul — Mike Galloway was inordinately fortunate not to become the third player to be ordered off in Aberdeen's last three Scottish Cup visits to Hampden. His first act on coming on as substitute was to deliver a ferocious tackle for which referee George Smith might well have selected a different shade of card.

The substitutes came on, the game drifted into extra time, both sides became less and less willing to attempt anything. Over the 120 minutes, it would perhaps be fair to say that Celtic had taken more from the match, if only because they had brought so little to it in the way of expectation. Once again, club tradition had enabled them to make the most of the poor hand they had been dealt. In any other year, they would have come back for the replay, buoyed up and fancying their chances the second time round.

Not this year. In an almost unnoticed decision, the S.F.A. had decreed that the final must be decided on the day by kicks from the penalty mark so that when at the end of two hours, George Smith's whistle resounded across a still-scoreless Hampden, the teams repaired to the centre-circle, the business of the afternoon still to be in a real sense begun.

There were the usual managerial exhortations, and the considerable amount of paper work that needs to be done before a penalty shoot-out can get under way. Celtic would take their penalties first, a considerable advantage but perhaps partly offset by the fact that the kicks were being taken at the end of the ground where the Aberdeen supporters were congregated. Almost immediately, Aberdeen were effectively ahead. Darius Wdowczyk was wide and high with his penalty and Theo Snelders could afford to watch it sail past. The Dons converted their own spot kick and briefly led.

It was not a lead they were to hold for very long. With the score at three all, including a Celtic miss, Brian Grant came up to take his kick and keep Aberdeen ahead. It was clear from his nervous approach and backward leaning that all was not well and it was not too surprising that the ball was scooped over the bar. Aberdeen had lost the benefit of the Wdowczyk miss and were now in a fearful position of taking penalty kicks to save the game, for every time Celtic scored, the Parkhead team would now be in the lead.

183

The statutory five penalties came and went, the sides level at 4-4. It was now the turn of the second-rank takers to step up and right well did they respond to the mounting tension. Not all the players were affected by this tension to the same degree of course, for goalkeepers, although nervous, can really only be heroes in the context of a penalty shoot-out. If they are beaten from the spot, then they are blameless and if they effect a save, they have very possibly gained the day for their side.

On two men the pressure was particularly severe. Picture the position of Charlie Nicholas as he stepped up to take his penalty. An ex-Celt and already widely rumoured to be going back to Parkhead, he would have been the target for every malicious pub tongue had he failed at this juncture. It is a mark of his cool professionalism that he slotted the ball away as if at the sideshow of a fair. For Joe Miller, the reverse was true; as a former Don it would be awkward if he were the one to let them off the hook now. He too was equal to the challenge.

So it went on until yet another half-hour had been consumed. The standard of penalty-taking was very high, normally tucked away into the corner with just occasionally the ball that bisected the goal-posts and would certainly have been stopped, had the goalkeeper not already gambled and plunged to one side or the other.

Eventually, it came to 8-8 on penalties and there seemed no good reason why the teams should not become the Flying Dutchmen of football, condemned to stay out there for ever taking successful penalties. The remaining handful of players who had still to go were visibly dreading being called forward, even so good a shot as Jackie Dziekanowski had ostentatiously failed to catch his skipper's eye for a time. At last it came the turn of the Celtic number three, Anton Rogan. As he prepared to take the kick, Theo Snelders in goal was whipping up the Aberdeen support in a collective frenzy of prayers for a miss.

Then, in an eerie silence, Rogan spotted the ball with obsessive care, measured his run and prepared to shoot. In fact, it was one of the best shots of the protracted session, low down towards Theo Snelders' left-hand post, but a foot or so too near to the keeper. Even so, his spring to turn the well-struck ball round the post was a save of the highest calibre and could truthfully be called brilliant goalkeeping rather than any major fault on the part of the kicker.

1990 ABERDEEN v. CELTIC. Theo Snelders appears to be asking the Aberdeen support how they liked his save from Anton Rogan's penalty.

Out on the park all was Bedlam. The Aberdeen fans were dancing and hugging each other, his colleagues were doing the same office for Theo Snelders. Distraught, Rogan sank to the turf, head buried in his hands, oblivious to the consoling pats administered by his team-mates. Only Pat Bonner moved briskly to his goal-line. He had work to do if possible. Aberdeen had not scored THEIR penalty yet, as far as he was concerned all that had happened was that Celtic had missed one.

All eyes turned to the Aberdeen kicker, Brian Irvine, the number five, young and although now a first-team regular, comparatively inexperienced. There was not an Aberdeen supporter there who did not remember that in a similar situation in Germany, even the great Willie Miller had missed crucially from the spot. Afterwards, the young man said that in the turmoil of the moment, he thought of the message which he had received from the elders of the Deeside Christian Fellowship Church, a message which simply stated "You'll never walk alone". With apparent total calm, Irvine made up his mind what to do and approached the ball on the spot. Pat Bonner was equally obviously seeking divine assistance which he would claim was vouchsafed to him a few weeks later in Italy.

But this was to be Brian Irvine's day. Quietly, without any flourish, he sent a shoulder-high shot past the despairing Celtic goalkeeper and the celebrations could begin. In the middle of the on-field rejoicings, the figure of Alex McLeish could be seen making the rounds of every Celtic player, unfeignedly sympathising with them over the way the victory had been dashed from their hands after a most gallant and protracted resistance.

There was much discussion afterwards over the method of settlement. It had certainly imposed a severe additional strain on the players. Brian Irvine was quoted as saying "I know that it wasn't my strength that kicked the ball into the net. God was beside me and helping me". Many supporters felt that the method chosen was unsatisfactory in that it inevitably landed an individual player with the tag of being the man whose miss had cost the club the Cup. They argued that such a miss in the normal run of play was a perfectly acceptable burden for a professional footballer to carry but that in the artificial circumstances of a penalty shoot-out, it was an imposition which was

Twin heroes — Snelders and Irvine.

too great to bear. If the game had to be settled on the day, then corner kicks were a better way of doing it since they reflected more accurately the course which the match had taken.

Their opponents maintained that those who went to a final were entitled to see a result on the day, both on the grounds of expense - a cogent argument where Aberdeen were concerned - and on the fact that replays were seldom matches to capture the imagination. At the end of the day, all that perhaps could be said was that the competition had been decided by rule and that Aberdeen had emerged as winners.

Celtic had the minor but real consolation that they had performed very well on the day and that in the middle of a trough, they had been capable of extending Aberdeen to the utmost. Their manager, Billy McNeill, was rightly pleased with the efforts of his staff.

"I have no complaints whatever about the attitude and application of my players. I thought that they worked extremely hard and that we had the edge overall."

As for Aberdeen, it was back to the triumphant return to the city and the reception which had become so much a part of recent years. The club had won two trophies, major trophies at that, in what would have seemed at first to be a season for regrouping and for new manager and players to get to know each other.

For a time, there seemed a threat of further major disruptions of the playing staff. Charlie Nicholas had done a good job for the Dons without ever giving the impression that Pittodrie was where his heart finally lay. There had been the hope that the arrival of the cultured and lethal Gillhaus might spur him into re-signing but it was not to be. He had provided many delightful flashes of skill for the Aberdeen support and now was going back to the ground and club where he had started out.

In the summer months which followed the Hampden success, there was the probability that the departing Nicholas would be joined by Alex McLeish and Jim Bett, but happily any outstanding differences were resolved and the two decided to continue their careers at Pittodrie. This was highly important not only for the intrinsic value of the two men concerned, but because it is vital, even in these days of freedom of contract, that

It's all over. The victorious Aberdeen side of 1990.

Aberdeen F.C. is not seen simply as a staging-post on the road to higher things.

Both men were elected Player of the Year, McLeish by the Scottish Football Writers and Bett by his fellow professionals. It was not in Alex Smith's nature to be over-flamboyantly demonstrative but even he would have had to assess the Dons latest Scottish Cup success as "no' bad". The measure of their achievement was that the side they had beaten, Celtic, would now be out of European competition for the first time in 12 years. As their manager Billy McNeill had foreseen, appetite grows by what it feeds on and it has certainly proved so for Aberdeen Football Club.

1990 — ALEX McLEISH REMEMBERS

The 1990 match against Celtic was my fifth Scottish Cup Final and of course I had scored in my first one against Rangers in 1982. I have vivid memories of the goal because I don't score too many. We had forced a corner kick which was partially cleared. Neale Simpson had a shot blocked and the ball came my way. It was almost dead as it got to me and I could see that it was falling perfectly for the curved shot. As soon as it left my boot I knew that Jim Stewart had to be in difficulties and it curled into the top corner of the next. That got us back into the game and we won comfortably in extra time. We buried a myth that day at Hampden that provincial teams couldn't win in Scottish Cup finals against the Old Firm. We had won the championship in 1980 but nothing since so the Scottish Cup success was very sweet.

The next year, 1983, again against Rangers was lucky for me in one way in that I had no problem in raising myself after Gothenburg. The reason was that I had injured myself in the next League game against Hibernian and it was very doubtful if I would make the final. I had clattered my knee off an advertising board at the edge of the track. Normally the Cup Final team was announced on the Monday previous but I was really struggling then and the team was held over as late as the Thursday. Even then I thought I couldn't make it but Fergie wasn't a great man for over-sympathising and he said that with an injection and a good strapping I'd be alright and he was spot on as he often was.

You forget the injury during the game and I played quite well, considering. I was late coming back to the dressing-room, I'd been caught up with the fans and talking to some of our invalid supporters and came into the dressing-room screaming with joy and excitement. Then I noticed the place was deathly quiet. "What's up?" I asked and Gordon Strachan said "Och, the ...... manager's going off his head." I think Fergie blew up at us because he set such high standards for us.

After our first win in 1982 I think Fergie realised how good this particular Aberdeen team could be. I remember his saying "The sky's the limit for this team, don't ever doubt yourself." He wanted to master the Old Firm as a manager in the same way that he wanted us to master them as players. He

1990 ABERDEEN v. CELTIC. It's all over. Brian Irvine has tucked away the crucial penalty kick and is here being congratulated by team-mates Theo Snelders and Robert Connor.

taught us to have a good conceit of ourselves, and when we went away with Scotland teams, to make ourselves noticed, not to sit in a corner in the shadow of the Old Firm players.

Gothenburg convinced us that we were a good side. That started in the tunnel before the match when Alex Ferguson said "Out there and let's hear you shout!" We shouted a bit in the tunnel and a couple of the Real Madrid players shouted back in imitation of us as a bit of a joke but you could see that they were just a bit apprehensive.

The 1990 final was strange in some ways. I don't really think the win at Parkhead a few days before the final made much difference if only because quite a few Aberdeen players that night were not going to be playing on the Saturday. There was some daft comment in the press on the lines of "If this is what Aberdeen Reserves can do to Celtic, what will the first team do?" But of course it rarely works out like that. Celtic are always a tricky proposition. They keep attacking almost always, though I can remember one match at Pittodrie where they won 1-0 after defending most of the game. I think Frank McGarvie got their goal that day.

We were certainly expected to win in the 1990 final. Earlier in the Cup there had been a great deal of paper talk about what Hearts Tiny Terrors, John Robertson and Scott Crabbe, would do to us in the cup-tie at Pittodrie. We just let the hype go and trained hard and on the day we demolished Hearts 4-0. I think in the final the same thing may have happened to us. Everybody told us we would win easily and we never quite got our game together. I think we were lulled just a wee bit for this game. Celtic played very hard, that was understandable, for not only was it the final but it was their last chance of a European place for the following season. But they did not quite click as a football side.

The game was anything but a classic, I think we were all very aware that it could go to penalties, certainly there wasn't a great deal of attacking in the extra half-hour.

We didn't have any closely-worked out list of penalty takers, we felt it better not to put too much strain on young players too far in advance. Jim Bett would take an early kick, he was the normal penalty man, and the forwards were asked to go early as well. But we were looking for volunteers, and I can't remember anyone hiding away as the kicks progressed. When

Brian Grant missed with his kick we were really in trouble as we were now going second and had to score with every penalty just to keep alive. I therefore thought it was up to me - a senior player - to take responsibility.

Strangely I wasn't half as fired up about taking the penalty myself as I get watching other players taking them. I remember asking the referee if I could spot the ball myself and he said yes. I also told myself to take a long run at the ball, most of the penalties I've seen missed have been because the kicker took too short a run. I made up my mind where I was putting the ball and walked back. I had never been out of the papers for about a week because I had won the Player of the Year from the Football Writers and all I could think of was, "If I miss, here is where the Player of the Year gets egg all over his face." Packy Bonner guessed correctly which way I would hit it but the shot was too powerful for him and of course the shoot-out went on until Anton Rogan missed and Brian Irvine scored.

On second thoughts I don't really think Anton Rogan missed. It was a well-struck penalty and if you look at the video you will see how good Theo Snelders' save was, there's a hand like a shovel shooting out at the left-hand post to turn the ball round. In my experience fans are quick to forgive players who miss a penalty kick in such one-off situations whereas I still get stick for my short pass-back in the game against Real Madrid in Gothenburg.

This was the first time we had won a Scottish Cup under Alex Smith. He is quieter than Alex Ferguson, but can be quite spectacular if he thinks we've done something wrong. Whereas Fergie used to knock us down and Archie Knox picked us up, nowadays it's the manager who smoothes us over usually after Jockie Scott has done the nebbing!

Over the years we learned to survive the opening all-out attack from the Old Firm when we met them at Hampden. Rangers today will still throw everything at you in League matches at Ibrox but when they come to Pittodrie they tend to be more cautious. It had always been difficult for Aberdeen to win in Glasgow, the odds are stacked against us, and it will become even more difficult if people stop travelling as a result of live satellite television. It is very difficult for Aberdeen supporters to get to Hampden Park for an evening kick-off, with the possibility of an eight o'clock start, extra time and penalties, and perhaps not returning to Aberdeen until 2 in the morning. You need a lift from a big Aberdeen support.

After the Celtic match I did make a point of consoling Celtic players, that's true, I've been there before and know what it's like to lose a penalty shoot-out in a big match. I haven't really thought about whether corners would be better. The fans like penalties but it's a bit heart-stopping for the players.

CHAPTER FOURTEEN

LOOKING BACK

By the normal chronological standards of football, Aberdeen's association with Scottish Cup finals is comparatively brief, extending as it does to little more than half a century. In that time, however, the progress made by the northern club has been little short of staggering.

On that first visit to Hampden in 1937, the atmosphere was one of a country outing to the big city. It was a great occasion precisely because of its rarity and while it would have been nice to win, there was a sense in which the qualifying to be there was the all-important thing. As it happened, that day the club was to participate in the last of the Cup finals where a really massive crowd was in attendance.

The Aberdeen support has often been castigated in the Press, just occasionally by the players themselves, for being subdued and comparatively undemonstrative. The other side to this has been a more gracious acceptance of defeat than is found elsewhere in Scotland. The support was very understanding in 1937 and equally and more importantly so, as late as 1978.

Inevitably in a short-span competition such as the Scottish Cup, inequalities will emerge. It is quite possible to win the trophy without having encountered serious opposition until the semi-final stage. Equally, in recent years, the path to Hampden may involve three away matches with Premier Division clubs and then another such on a neutral ground in the semi-final. Ability and commitment to the Pittodrie cause have therefore not always been even-handedly rewarded. No one worked harder for the Dons than Jackie Hather or Fred Martin, but not one of their three visits to the Scottish Cup final ended in success.

Compare that with the managerial record of Alex Ferguson who four times took his team to the final and four times emerged bearing away the trophy. Take the even more remarkable case of Alex McLeish who has not known defeat in his five Scottish Cup finals. The years have seen a changing situation for Aberdeen. Until the 1980s, a Scottish Cup final was something to be reached every five years or so at most, with defeat in the last stage an almost constant companion. Today, it is as much a subject for remark if Aberdeen do not make the final as thirty years ago it was when they did. The club is well run; there is a system discernible which can survive frequent changes of manager and the new threat, not of course an exclusive threat to Aberdeen, of freedom of contract.

Aberdeen have elbowed themselves into a position in which they can claim with perfect validity that the Big Two in Scottish football has now become the Big Three. In some ways, their performance is more creditable than that of their rivals because nowadays with the Old Firm, the development of a home-grown player is a novelty indeed. At Pittodrie, however, not only have several highly-gifted European players come to join the club, but there is a constant stream of young aspirants pushing through from the junior sides. No sooner does a David Robertson or a Brian Irvine establish himself than there is another surge from the Gregg Watsons and Eoin Jesses of the world.

This is not necessarily a situation that will continue indefinitely. When clubs held the registrations of players in a vice-like grip, there was a case for nurturing home-grown talent, indeed it was essential that this should be done. Freedom of contract entails the very real risk that the club which does all the painstaking nursery work may very well not be the club which derives the greatest benefit from the matured player.

Life will never be easy for Aberdeen. There is a certain geographical isolation even as we approach 2000 A.D., which will sometimes tell against their best efforts to attract players.

Many a highly-skilled Glaswegian begins to experience home-sickness as he drives through Baillieston traffic lights! In many areas, however, the Dons have shown themselves to be almost our most forward-thinking club. The stadium has been all seated for several years now, with a consequent improvement in crowd behaviour. The author used to have friendly disputes with the late and great Chris Anderson about this. Chris would argue that baseball was free of crowd violence because the spectators were all seated; the author's belief was that baseball remained trouble-free because of the total absence of travelling support.

It is not only in the way of provision of amenities that Aberdeen have pioneered the way. It could well be argued that over the last ten years or so, it has been the performance of Aberdeen in European competition (together with that of Dundee United) which has kept Scottish club football credible in the wider international sphere.

With some claim to be considered the Scottish side of the 1980s, the task ahead of Aberdeen is to maintain that standard for what remains of the century. A great psychological blow has been struck with the successful retention of Alex McLeish and Jim Bett. It is not only that they are fine players in their own right, but the knock-on beneficial effect is incalculable. If these two international players have thought it worthwhile effectively to end their days at Pittodrie, then there is likely to be a perceptible effect on younger players of comparable ability.

Should that be so, then it is certain that over the next few years, the wagons will roll southwards in large numbers on May mornings to see Aberdeen as they attempt to improve on what is already a distinguished Scottish Cup record and another Final Edition brings its news of triumph or failure.

APPENDIX A

ABERDEEN IN SCOTTISH CUP FINALS

1937 - Aberdeen 1 Celtic 2

ABERDEEN: Johnstone; Cooper, Temple, Dunlop, Falloon, Thomson, Beynon, MacKenzie, Armstrong, Mills, Lang.

CELTIC: Kennoway; Hogg, Morrison, Geatons, Lyon, Paterson, Delaney, Buchan, McGrory, Crum, Murphy.

REFEREE: M Hutton (Glasgow)

SCORERS: Aberdeen: Armstrong
     Celtic: Crum, Buchan

ABERDEEN MANAGER: Paddy Travers

1947 - Aberdeen 2 Hibernian 1

ABERDEEN: Johnstone; McKenna, Taylor, McLaughlin, Dunlop, Waddell, Harris, Hamilton, Williams, Baird, McCall.

HIBERNIAN: Kerr; Govan, Shaw, Howie, Aird, Kean, Smith, Finnegan, Cuthbertson, Turnbull, Ormond.

REFEREE: R Calder (Rutherglen)

SCORERS: Aberdeen: Hamilton, Williams
     Hibernian: Cuthbertson

ABERDEEN MANAGER: Dave Halliday

1953 - Aberdeen 1 Rangers 1

ABERDEEN: Martin; Mitchell, Shaw, Harris, Young,

Allister, Rodger, Yorston, Buckley, Hamilton, Hather.

RANGERS: Niven; Young, Little, McColl, Stanners, Pryde, Waddell, Grierson, Paton, Prentice, Hubbard.

REFEREE: J A Mowat (Burnside)

SCORERS: Aberdeen: Yorston
             Rangers: Prentice

REPLAY - Aberdeen 0 Rangers 1

ABERDEEN: Martin; Mitchell, Shaw, Harris, Young, Allister, Rodger, Yorston, Buckley, Hamilton, Hather.

RANGERS: Niven; Young, Little, McColl, Woodburn, Pryde, Waddell, Grierson, Simpson, Paton, Hubbard.

REFEREE: J A Mowat (Burnside)

SCORER: Rangers: Simpson

ABERDEEN MANAGER: Dave Halliday

1954 - Aberdeen 1 Celtic 2

ABERDEEN: Martin; Mitchell, Caldwell, Allister, Young, Glen, Leggat, Hamilton, Buckley, Clunie, Hather.

CELTIC: Bonnar; Haughney, Meechan, Evans, Stein, Peacock, Higgins, Fernie, Fallon, Tully, Mochan.

REFEREE: C E Faultless (Glasgow)

SCORERS: Aberdeen: Buckley
             Celtic: Young, Fallon (own goal)

ABERDEEN MANAGER: Dave Halliday

1959 - Aberdeen 1 St Mirren 3

ABERDEEN: Martin; Caldwell, Hogg, Brownlee, Clunie, Glen, Ewen, Davidson, Baird, Wishart, Hather.

ST MIRREN: Walker; Lapsley, Wilson, Neilson, McGugan, Leishman, Rodger, Bryceland, Baker, Gemmell, Miller.

REFEREE: J A Mowat (Burnside)

SCORERS: Aberdeen: Baird
                  St Mirren: Bryceland, Miller, Baker

ABERDEEN MANAGER: Davie Shaw

1967 - Aberdeen 0 Celtic 2

ABERDEEN: Clark; Whyte, Shewan, Munro, McMillan, Petersen, Wilson, Smith, Storrie, Melrose, Johnston.

CELTIC: Simpson; Craig, Gemmell, Murdoch, McNeill, Clark, Johnstone, Wallace, Chalmers, Auld, Lennox.

REFEREE: W M Syme (Glasgow)

SCORERS: Celtic: Wallace (2)

ABERDEEN MANAGER: Eddie Turnbull

1970 - Aberdeen 3 Celtic 1

ABERDEEN: Clark; Boel, Murray, Hermiston, McMillan, M. Buchan, McKay, Robb, Forrest, Harper, Graham. Substitute: G. Buchan.

CELTIC: Williams; Hay, Gemmell, Murdoch, McNeill, Brogan, Johnstone, Wallace, Connelly, Lennox, Hughes. Substitute: Auld.

REFEREE: R H Davidson (Airdrie)

SCORERS: Aberdeen: Harper (penalty), McKay (2)
                  Celtic: Lennox

ABERDEEN MANAGER: Eddie Turnbull

1978   Aberdeen 1 Rangers 2

ABERDEEN: Clark; Kennedy, Ritchie, McMaster, Garner, Miller, Sullivan, Fleming (Scanlon), Harper, Jarvie, Davidson.

RANGERS: McCloy; Jardine, Greig, Forsyth, Jackson, MacDonald, McLean, Russell, Johnstone, Smith, Cooper.

REFEREE: B R McGinlay (Balfron)

SCORERS: Aberdeen: Ritchie
                  Rangers: MacDonald, Johnstone

ABERDEEN MANAGER: Billy McNeill

1982 - Aberdeen 4 Rangers 1 (after extra time)

ABERDEEN: Leighton; Kennedy, Rougvie, McMaster (Bell), McLeish, Miller, Strachan, McGhee, Cooper, Simpson, Hewitt (Black).

RANGERS: Stewart; Jardine (McAdam), Dawson, McClelland, Jackson, Bett, Cooper, Russell, Dalziel (McLean), Miller, McDonald.

REFEREE: B R McGinlay (Balfron)

SCORERS: Aberdeen: McLeish, McGhee, Strachan, Cooper
            Rangers: McDonald

ABERDEEN MANAGER: Alex Ferguson

1983 - Aberdeen 1 Rangers 0 (after extra time)

ABERDEEN: Leighton; Rougvie (Watson), McMaster, Cooper, McLeish, Miller, Strachan, Simpson, McGhee, Black, Weir (Hewitt).

RANGERS: McCloy; Dawson, McClelland, McPherson, Paterson, Bett, Cooper (Davies), McKinnon, Clark, Russell, McDonald (Dalziel).

REFEREE: D Syme (Rutherglen)

SCORER: Aberdeen: Black

ABERDEEN MANAGER: Alex Ferguson

1984 - Aberdeen 2 Celtic 1 (after extra time)

ABERDEEN: Leighton; McKimmie, Rougvie (Stark), Cooper, McLeish, Miller, Strachan, Simpson, McGhee, Black, Weir (Bell).

CELTIC: Bonner; McGrain, Reid (Melrose), Aitken, W McStay, McLeod, Provan, P McStay, McGarvey, Burns, McClair (Sinclair).

REFEREE: R B Valentine (Dundee)

SCORERS: Aberdeen: Black, McGhee
            Celtic: P McStay

ABERDEEN MANAGER: Alex Ferguson

1986 - Aberdeen 3 Heart of Midlothian 0

ABERDEEN: Leighton; McKimmie, McQueen, McMaster (Stark), McLeish, W. Miller, Hewitt (J Miller), Cooper, McDougall, Bett, Weir.

HEARTS: Smith; Kidd, Whittaker, Jardine, Berry, Levein, Colquhoun, Black, Clark, MacKay, Robertson.

REFEREE: H Alexander (Kilmarnock)

SCORERS: Aberdeen: Hewitt (2), Stark

ABERDEEN MANAGER: Alex Ferguson

1990 - Aberdeen 0 Celtic 0 (after extra time)
Aberdeen won 9-8 on penalties

ABERDEEN: Snelders; McKimmie, Robertson, Grant, McLeish, Irvine, Nicholas, Bett, Mason, Connor, Gillhaus. Substitutes: Watson, Jess.

CELTIC: Bonner; Wdowczyk, Rogan, Grant, Elliott, Whyte, Stark, McStay, Dziekanowski, Walker, Miller. Substitutes: Coyne, Galloway.

REFEREE: G B Smith (Edinburgh)

SCORERS: No scoring

ABERDEEN MANAGER: Alex Smith

APPENDIX B

ABERDEEN GOALSCORERS IN SCOTTISH CUP FINALS

Two goals	E Black
	J Hewitt
	M McGhee
	D McKay
One goal	M Armstrong
	H Baird
	P Buckley
	N Cooper
	G Hamilton
	J Harper
	A McLeish
	S Ritchie
	W Stark
	G Strachan
	S Williams
	H Yorston

APPENDIX C

THREE OR MORE CUP FINAL APPEARANCES

Five appearances	A McLeish
	W Miller
Four appearances	N Cooper
	G Hamilton (including replay)
	J Hather (including replay)
	J Leighton
Three appearances	E Black
	R Clark
	J Hewitt
	F Martin
	M McGhee
	S McKimmie
	J McMaster
	N Simpson

Bob Crampsey is one of the best-known broadcasters on the sporting scene in Scotland and is widely acknowledged as the game's leading historian. His books include the official Centenary History of the Scottish Football League and that of Queen's Park Football Club, while three of his novels have sporting backgrounds in cricket, athletics and association football respectively. He has worked for many years with BBC Scotland, Scottish Television and Radio Clyde.

In 1965, he won the BBC Brain of Britain contest and in 1972/73 was a semi-finalist on Mastermind.